Henry's Dream

The Life Story of Henry Wharton
*Former British, European and
Commonwealth Champion*

Jim Kirkwood

Foreword by Bob Mee

Dalcumly Press

First published in the UK in 2014

Dalcumly Press
10 Forest Grove
Kilmarnock, Ayrshire KA3 1UP

ISBN 978-0-9569253-2-9

Papers used in this book are natural, renewable and recyclable products sourced from well-managed forests and certified in accordance with the rules of the Forest Stewardship Council.

Typeset in Adobe Garamond, designed and produced by Gilmour Print, www.self-publish-books.co.uk

Henry would like to dedicate this book
to his mother, father, brother Eddie,
his wife Amanda and his children.
Also to Bill Brown, Dennie Mancini,
Terry Lawless, Terry O'Neil, Mickey Duff,
Gary Atkin and life long friend
Ron Hopley who have all been
with him through this journey.

Contents

Foreword

When Jim Kirkwood asked me to write the foreword for his book on Henry Wharton I considered it a privilege to get the chance to pay tribute to one of the most talented boxers of his generation. Henry was a quiet man and an honest professional who won British, Commonwealth and European titles and came close three times to adding that 'world champion' tag to his name. If he had achieved that, nobody would have deserved it more.

I remember Wharton first in the late 1980s when he was a part of an England amateur team that included men like Richie Woodhall, Henry Akinwande, Neville Brown, Robert McCracken. His power was evident then. He stopped Ray Close in the first round in an England-Ireland international in Milton Keynes and in an away match in Poland, when the Polish team contained future stars like Andrew Golota and Dariusz Michalczewski, Henry was England's star as he destroyed a middleweight named Bogdan Wieczorak in the first round.

He missed out on the Seoul Olympics but when he turned professional in September 1989 it was obvious that his economical, intelligent, aggressive style and beautifully delivered left hook would serve him well as he developed. Mickey Duff gave him time to learn on quality undercards at Wembley and in Yorkshire at places like Dewsbury Sports Centre and, a little later, the Barbican Centre in his home city of York. Henry learned his job with Terry O'Neill and Gary

Atkin – perhaps not the most fashionable coaches in the country, but then Henry was about what worked for him, not fashion or reputation. He knew how good they were and how important it was to have someone you trust, and who knows you, in the corner at the end of each round.

From 1991 when he won the Commonwealth super-middleweight title by outpointing the tough, rugged Australian, Rod Carr, until the end of his career seven years later, he was a high profile, world class operator, but there was never a chance that he would let success go to his head. He just wasn't that type.

In the first of his three world championship attempts, against Nigel Benn at Earls Court, London, in February 1994, there were plenty of critics who felt his big left hook could wreak havoc with Benn's defences. As it was, a Jimmy Tibbs-inspired Benn forsook his 'Dark Destroyer' reputation for the night and concentrated on making as few mistakes as possible through the 12 absorbing rounds. Benn won on points, but two judges had Wharton only a couple of points behind at the final bell.

He was unlucky to meet Chris Eubank on a night when Chris produced one of the finest performances of his career at the G-Mex arena in Manchester in December 1994. I had been in South Africa for Eubank's previous WBO super-middleweight defence when he scraped past a so-so American named Dan Schommer with the help of some extremely generous judging. Eubank was horribly weight-drained and if he had faced Henry Wharton on that night, there is no doubt in my mind that he would have lost by a distance. I'd have tipped Wharton to dispose of Schommer any day, anywhere.

However, the British Board of Control took such a dim view of Eubank's preparations that they forced him to have his weight-making for the Wharton fight monitored carefully. This was a hot topic at the time with medical officials working hard to educate boxers, trainers, managers and promoters over the dangers of reducing weight too quickly. The consequence of their close scrutiny was that Eubank prepared meticulously, spurred on too by the fact that he was well aware that Henry posed a far greater threat than Schommer ever could.

With hindsight it was the last of Eubank's big victories – he was to lose the title to Steve Collins in County Cork in his next fight. Wharton put on a gritty, determined display, had his moments but was behind by between two and six points on the cards at the end.

Victories over men like Mauro Galvano, Sam Storey and the eccentric, awkward Vincenzo Nardiello kept him in the spotlight, and brought him the European title, before the third of his world title fights, against Robin Reid in what was then called the Nynex Arena, Manchester, in May 1997, brought the frustration of another points setback. It was no comfort to him then, and probably isn't now, that the powerful Reid focused on using his boxing skills rather than getting involved and risking standing toe-to-toe. One judge had it level at the end, but the other two had Reid well clear.

I saw Wharton last on the Lennox Lewis-Shannon Briggs heavyweight title show in the cavernous Boardwalk Hall in Atlantic City in March 1998. It was Henry's American debut and he outpointed a light-heavyweight named Franklin Edmondson.

There was only one more fight, fittingly back at home in York, six months later and he decided that at the none-too-advanced age of 30, he would leave it at that. His three defeats in a 31-fight career had all come in world title fights and in that time nobody ever looked like stopping him.

Wharton was never one to beat his chest and tell the world what he would or wouldn't do. He just got one with his job. And for nine years of what was a hugely entertaining era in British boxing he did that job exceptionally well.

It's good to know that in retirement he's still involved in the sport, passing on his knowledge to aspiring amateurs in his gym in a renovated cinema in the Acomb area of York.

I'd like to thank him for the entertainment he gave all those years ago and take this opportunity to wish him well for the future, and I'm sure that after his previous books on Dave Charnley and Tony Sibson, Jim Kirkwood will do Henry Wharton's story full justice.

Bob Mee, *9 May 2014*

Acknowledgements

You can't write a book like this without help, and I'm very much indebted to several people who have given up their time, very willingly, to assist me with the project.

It becomes exceedingly difficult to piece together details for a biography without the active assistance of the subject. Henry Wharton answered every telephone call, attended every meeting, and answered every question posed, without hesitation and with great enthusiasm. He was always open, forthright and factually accurate with his recollections, which made my task so much easier.

Almost all the photographs in this book are provided by Nigel Holland, for whom the photographing of Henry's career was so much more than a mere occupational task. Yes, Nigel was working for local and national newspapers, but he'd also become a close personal friend. His archives of Henry's fights, training sessions, family life and public appearances would be a worthy platform for a purely photographic book on their own. I'd like to record my thanks to Nigel for his kind assistance.

Bob Mee is a renowned boxing historian and journalist. What he doesn't know about British boxing over the last thirty to forty years, is not worth knowing. Once again, like his previous help with my book on Tony Sibson, Bob has willingly provided the foreword, which I'm sure adds a bit of class to the final offering. Thanks Bob, you're a gentleman.

Henry's mum, was the first person I spoke to after Henry

himself, and she very ably outlined the early Wharton family life on the road. Although not a traveller herself, she quickly settled into that lifestyle, and is proud of the way she raised her family and the friends she made. Janet painstakingly collected every newspaper article and photograph she could find on Henry's boxing career, pasted them into albums in chronological order, and these provided invaluable assistance to me in my research. I'm in her debt.

Terry O'Neill is one of these men who are becoming increasingly rare in that his life has been almost totally devoted to boxing. He's done it all, both in the amateur and professional scenes. From helping to create St Patrick's amateur boxing club in Leeds, to coaching the England team at the Commonwealth games, identifying and training numerous champions, right the way through to managing Henry up until the Benn fight. Sadly, Terry and Henry haven't spoken for years, though neither remember ever falling out, or saying a harsh word about each other. Terry easily set aside any issues that might have existed and provided detailed information, including documentary evidence, of Henry's days as a young amateur at St Pat's and the first stage of his professional career. Thanks Terry, you were a great help.

Ron Hopley has been a true friend to Henry for almost thirty years, having first met him while they were training at St Pat's in Leeds. Ron provided the 'other' side of Henry's life away from the boxing ring, and his stories demonstrated that he was just like the rest of us when away from the spartan environment of the training camp. Ron was a professional boxer himself and still travels a considerable distance from his home in Ripon to York three nights a week to assist with the coaching at Henry's Gym.

Gary Atkin has been everything to Henry. Coach, trainer, advisor, chauffeur, sparring partner, jogging partner, but most importantly – a friend. Gary was the first person Henry met when he arrived at St Patrick's for the first time in the early 80s and they've never been apart since. Gary provided all the factual information a writer could ever need from then on, including dates, times, personalities, and importantly gave a unique view of life behind the scenes for a championship level boxer. Gary was another who never failed to answer a phone call or respond to an email, and quite readily invited a complete stranger into his family home, without a second thought. It was much appreciated.

Isaac Inns, who was a club mate of Henry in his early days at the York Amateur Boxing Club, Denzil Browne long time spar mate and friend, as well as Nick Manners, all added their recollections.

It was really important to get a consistent flavour of how Henry's exploits in the ring were being received locally, and this was made all the more accessible through articles in the Yorkshire Evening Press/Post.

Finally, but probably most importantly, I have again to thank Douglas Gilmour at Gilmour Print, for putting my words and photographs together to produce another book which has at least the appearance of being professional on the outside! If the content matches the exterior I'll be quite happy.

If I've forgotten anybody it's an unintentional oversight, sorry in advance!

Introduction

Henry's Dream was actually three dreams – to win the Amateur Boxing Association (ABA) title, to represent GB at the Olympics and to become the world champion as a professional. The other side of that particular coin was the nightmares, from which he'd wake up in a panic having imagined he was entering the ring unfit and unready.

Henry Wharton set himself high targets and was determined to drive himself to achieve them. In just under one hundred amateur contests and thirty one in the paid ranks, there were perhaps only two occasions when his nightmares became reality, as a star amateur in Prague and in his last fight over ten years later.

The dreams began in the unlikely surroundings of a gypsy caravan site as he watched his older brothers step out towards the local amateur boxing club, and became more ingrained when his father, Billy, would tell him, "you'll be a world champion one day, my lad."

Henry's father wasn't just extolling words of encouragement. He'd some basis for his comments. Tony Murray, who still assists Wharton with coaching duties at his own club almost thirty five years later, saw the early signs that he'd a special talent. "I was a bit older than Henry and maybe had around twenty or so fights myself. I remember watching this young gypsy lad shadow boxing and hitting the heavy bag, and he looked like he'd been in the gym for years. In fact he'd just started. He was a natural, and this was before I realised he could punch." His first coach, Bill Brown, saw the same.

We'll learn as we go along how Wharton came to be recognised as a huge puncher, but this early indication that he'd an 'eye' for boxing with good movement and timing should make us aware that there was more to him. But, there's no getting away from the fact that he had what all managers and promoters look for, a devastating ability to knock people out with great regularity.

Cruiserweight Denzil Browne from Leeds, was a very capable and experienced fighter and having sparred hundreds of hours with Wharton both as amateurs and professionals, is ideally placed to comment on his punching power. "I've been in with Frank Bruno, Pat Barrett, Christophe Tiozzo, all punchers, Ralf Rocchigiani, Henry Maske, I've been in with a load of punchers. I'd place him just behind Bruno, because Bruno put me down when I sparred with him, but he was a big heavyweight. Henry hurt me for a week with a body shot one time. I never told no one but I was in pain for a week. After a while when we became friendly I think he eased up a bit and just used me for my height really. Man, could he punch!"

As well as having natural ability, and being a lethal puncher, Wharton was tough. He could take it. In all his professional career he was only knocked down once, and of course he got back up. Whether it was the tough upbringing as a traveller, or simply something in his genes, we can only speculate. Henry told me this story on the golf course only because it was a conversation piece after he saw his usual playing partner on another fairway. "A couple of years ago we were in the final of a pairs tournament and the tie was due to be played on the Sunday. On the Friday I was working on a roof with my mate and he accidentally put one of the tools through the palm of my hand. The insides were sticking out. We went to the hospital and after we checked in a sign came up that the waiting time was something like five hours. I said, "I'm not waiting for that." So we went to a wool shop in town and I bought a needle and thread. I didn't know how to sew so I asked the woman how to do it. She thought I was going to stitch a bit of cloth or something. When I told her it was for my hand she put her hands over her ears and kept saying,' I'm not listening, I don't want to hear.' I went home and took a handful of ice out the freezer and when it'd melted I put a few stitches in and went back to work. Later on it got painful and I asked Jamie to contact the other pair to see if we could get the tie delayed for a week, but we couldn't. I bandaged it up, and we won the tournament. I felt great about that."

More importantly, perhaps, than his life as a boxer and the successes he had, is the fact that he's a good person. He's well spoken, mannerly, and would spend the time of day with anyone. He thinks the world of his family, and they think the world of him. Nothing seems to worry him for too long. He has his faults like everybody else. Everyone who knows him realises that if arrangements are made to meet at a certain time, then add on another half hour – at least! Organisation – forget it! He's very reluctant to talk bad about anyone, and I haven't yet found anyone who'd something bad to say about him. There might be a message there for everyone?

There might have been several other titles for the book, all equally appropriate. It could've been entitled, 'From Caravan to Caesar's Palace' in allusion to Wharton's journey from life as part of a travelling family to his accommodation for his second last fight in Atlantic City. Or perhaps something along the lines of, 'Never a Backward Step' or 'Tough as They Come', because these would've described exactly the type of boxer Henry turned out to be. It must've been a daunting prospect going into a fight with him knowing he'd just keep coming no matter what you threw at him.

How despairing it must be for Wharton to learn, after all these years, how his opponent's backroom staff saw the fights when he challenged for the world title. Nigel Benn's trainer thought that it was his man's best performance. Eubank's trainer believed that it was possibly his toughest fight, and Robin Reid himself has gone on record to say that Wharton was the hardest puncher he ever fought. As Henry would say with a smile on his face, "Why did they have to be at their best when they fought me, could they not have had a bad night?"

When fans discuss a boxer's career they usually debate what was the best performance, and perhaps the worst. There's a lot of factors to consider. How good was the opponent? Was a title at stake? Was the fight in the opponent's home turf? For me Henry's best was his second fight with the Australian Rod Carr in defence of his Commonwealth title. This fight seemed to epitomise everything that made Wharton such an exciting fighter. Carr was a very underestimated foe. Very strong, with a superb left jab. As the fight settled down, Henry found himself in real trouble, being caught repeatedly by the Aussie boxer, but he managed to turn it around in devastating fashion, showing heart, strength, determination and possessing a punch like a mule. The downside of the debate as far as I'm concerned, was only part of a fight, the first four rounds of his biggest night up until that point, against Nigel Benn, when he hardly landed a meaningful punch.

It was a pleasure to write this book, about such a decent individual, whose character hasn't been effected by his fame, and who now finds himself again involved in the boxing business, giving something back to the sport which established him, at his height, as a household name. I hope I've done his career justice, and you all enjoy the journey.

CHAPTER 1

Life as a Traveller

What would be considered a normal routine family life for people in 1960's Britain? There's been books and films made on the subject, but generally speaking the family home would be an up and down stairs local authority house with perhaps a small garden. Inside would be mum and dad, possibly a couple of children, a small black and white television in the corner and a coal fire. Most families by now had an indoor toilet with a bath but it's doubtful if many had a shower unit, a telephone or a refrigerator. A lot of fathers might be able to afford a small car and an annual summer holiday perhaps to Blackpool, Great Yarmouth, Bournemouth or Brighton.

This, however, was far removed from the circumstances into which baby Henry Wharton was born on 23 November 1967. Dad, Billy Wharton, was a gypsy and mum, Janet Wagstaff came from the more settled surroundings of Holbeck in Leeds. When Henry came along he already had six older brothers and sisters and the family lived the life of travellers, moving from campsite to campsite in their caravan in search of work. However on this occasion, awaiting the birth of her seventh child, Billy and Janet moved into a rented house near her former home and the baby was born in Leeds St Mary's Maternity hospital. The boy was named after grandfather Henry, a fully fledged Romany gypsy who used to entertain his family with old Maurice Chevalier songs.

As spring approached the family were off on their travels again to Wisbech were they spent most summers picking fruit and vegetables from morning till night. As mother Janet recalls, "With only two compartments, me and the girls slept like sardines in one, and all the boys were in the other. But they were happy times."

They might have worked long hours for little financial reward and lived in cramped conditions without the little luxuries which others were beginning to enjoy, but they certainly had their own proud standards. Cleanliness was demanded by Billy and Janet. Henry can remember all of them having to wash themselves outside every morning in basins filled with cold water regardless of the weather. In the winter time when the caravan was pulled into Mr Lambert's site in the outskirts of York at Fulford, the same routine continued, only this time it was usually the case that the ice on top of the buckets had to be broken before the soap and lathering did their job.

Henry can remember that he'd long admired his fathers jet black hair and wondered why his was golden brown. Dad Billy had the answer however. He told Henry and the others that to get their hair to grow darker they had to wash it every day. Young Henry, after lifting his dripping mop out of the freezing basin would often ask Billy if his hair was darker now, and of course this would always illicit a positive response.

This demand for cleanliness was demonstrated more forcibly on another occasion. Billy had gone to the pub for the night and when he left, another travelling family was on the site they were visiting. Billy didn't consider them to be true travelling stock and was reluctant for any of the family to be involved with them.

Nevertheless, when the cat's away . . . . Henry and his brother began to play around a bonfire the 'others' had lit and by the end of the night, having jumped through the flames and fell about the ashes they were well and truly black with soot. They crept into the caravan and went to bed in this state. When Billy returned the worse for drink he could smell the smoke and his temper got the better of him. Janet, fearing the worst, told him she'd put the kettle on and heat up some water, all to no avail. Henry and his sibling were dragged out of bed and thrown out the caravan and told to wash themselves in the snow. To this day Henry has never been colder.

Typically for some travellers, there always seemed to be horses around, usually to pull carts full of vegetables and fruit in the fields. Henry can remember his dad having one horse in particular which he really held in great affection. He'd often be offered money to sell it but always managed to resist the temptation. Jealousy however can be a terrible master. One morning Billy's pride and joy was lying dead at the foot of a small incline. When the vet arrived he suggested that the horse had died from a heart attack but Billy knew horses and surprisingly insisted that a post mortem be carried out. This showed that the animal had been killed due to a nail causing damage in its stomach. To those unfamiliar with horses it would have been easy to assume that it'd swallowed the offending object but Henry's father knew that horses grind all their food in their mouth and would have spat a nail out before it got any further. It is highly likely that an aggrieved horse 'fancier' put a tube down the horses throat and blew the nail into position with the full knowledge of the likely outcome. Such was the cruelty that existed in some sections of the travelling community.

As Henry got older the family regularly returned in the winter to the Fulford site. Mr Lambert, the landowner once had an orchard there, and turned it over for use by the travellers for a rent. There were only a few families who used the site and Janet remembers the trailers being organised in a sort of square and in the middle the children would play under the watchful eyes of the mothers from their caravan windows. Billy and Janet were not satisfied with just seven children, and after Henry came Dinah, Charlotte, Alfred and Anne.

When Henry was about thirteen years old he'd begun pestering his parents to let him join his older brothers Billy and Eddie at the York Amateur Boxing Club in North Street, then ran by Bill Brown. Janet remembers Henry as being a particularly active boy and the boxing club appealed to his idea of being always on the move. Eventually Janet had to cave in to the constant requests and let him go along. Dad Billy had boxed as an amateur in the army during his National Service and there'd always been a suggestion that grandfather Henry had also fought.

The York ABC was very typical of what clubs were like in those days before community funding initiatives became available. It was based in All Saints' Church Hall, and the building was virtually derelict. Henry can remember the rain coming in through the roof. The punch bags were old and bursting; the boxing gloves were still filled with horsehair a remnant from the 1940s; some of the skipping ropes were tied together and the smell of stale sweat mingled with dampness creating a unique atmosphere which would be familiar to young boxers from that era. However, all of this should not detract from the quality of the training, nor the enthusiasm shown by Bill Brown, Jack Harris, Pete Goodrich and the other coaches who voluntarily gave up their time. Bill Brown was a great believer in teaching the basics by repeating and repeating moves until they became second nature. Sparring each night was standard practice, not to spar would have been equivalent to attending football training without kicking a ball! Training nights were Monday, Wednesday and Friday and everyone, regardless of age, trained together.

Henry's friend, and fellow gypsy, Isaac Inns can remember him at the club. "Even at an early age Henry was intense with his boxing. I've got a press photo at that time taken when two actors from a local theatre came to get lessons from Bill Brown for a play involving bare-knuckle fighting. There were over a dozen of us including my brother and Henry's brother Eddie. We were all standing around looking at the camera but not Henry. He's got his gloves up, right hand covering the side of his head and a jab coming out perfectly and not even facing the camera man." Isaac too was there at Henry's first bout travelling in a car with Henry to a club called the Three B's in Bridlington.

Janet can remember the build up to that fight very clearly. "With having such a big family we didn't have a lot of money, but I found out that Henry had to wear shorts, suitable shoes and a maroon vest and these just had to be bought for him somehow. I went into York with my daughter and we bought a pair of football shorts and a pair of baseball boots, but we couldn't find anywhere that sold a maroon vest. By the time we got back to the site I didn't know what we would do. You couldn't believe it but that night one of my friend's husband, Jimmy Francis, came home and he was wearing a maroon vest. He gave it to us and I washed and ironed it and Henry wore it that night. It's a good job that Jimmy was a thin man!" The well dressed young Wharton won his fight that night and he proudly posed for photographs the following morning with his brothers and sisters – along with the priceless trophy.

Henry too has vivid memories of this first night. "I had been for four bouts, but for some reason or other, whether they were too heavy or I was too light the bouts never happened. Anyway this particular night I was keyed up as usual, I jumped on the scales and I was 6st 2lb and my opponent was 6st – I was 2lb heavier. My coach Bill Brown came to me and said, they're not taking the bout. I said, 'Oh no, not again.' I was speaking to my cousin Dean, who was always there, and I said well can I have my meal ticket? I was one of eleven children, you know, I was starving, and I said, can Dean have one? When we got the tickets we ran straight for a pie and peas. I was saying to Dean, you don't understand how good I feel. I feel good tonight, I'd have been really good tonight, this is the best I've ever felt. I got a tap on my shoulder and it was coach Bill Brown and it was as if it was slow motion, he said, 'they've took the fight'. Dean was jumping up and down and I couldn't move. I sat back in my chair. Dean saw my face and he said 'you've just been saying how good you feel'. I'll tell you honestly, all the nerves started again. I was twice as bad as I was before. I said 'I have just had pie and peas,' and he said 'come on, that's not my fault'. Anyway, off we go, and thankfully I won the fight."

When youngsters first start attending amateur boxing clubs

the coaches can usually tell very early on which ones are going to stick at it. In the same way, to the experienced eye, it is possible to identify someone who has a spark of natural ability. This was the case with Henry. Bill Brown always said that from very early on he could see that the young Wharton was 'special' and that he fought like a 'professional'. When asked to explain this comment Henry said, "I suppose Bill could see me hooking with both hands in close and in those days that was not how amateurs were supposed to box."

Another positive aspect to Henry's early career was his ability to knock his opponents out. When fourteen and fifteen year olds take part in contests there can be stoppages usually because one lad has been overwhelmed, but it is extremely rare, and some would say that's a good thing, to see youngsters counted out lying on their backs. Sadly for Henry's early opponents that was the position most found themselves in.

While at the York ABC Henry reckons he had around twenty contests, fighting at Hull, Newcastle, Bridlington, Leeds, Malton, Darlington, and other local venues he now forgets, with only three fights going the distance. Two of those were points defeats, and in the other he won the decision. The remainder ended with a stoppage victory for the York lad with the vast majority being clean knockouts.

As a consequence of his growing reputation as a 'puncher', it became difficult to match young Wharton. The amateur game exists in a closely knit community and the 'word was out 'on him. On many occasions Bill Brown had to accept fights with far more experienced boxers just to keep him active and often he'd feel the need to apologise to his young protege.

This raises the old argument within boxing circles about whether 'punchers' are born or made. It's very similar to the age old academic debate about 'nature versus nurture'. Are we genetically 'pre-programmed' before we're born, or do we became who we are through interacting with the world as we grow up? In a boxing sense therefore, are concussive boxers born with this natural ability, or can it be learned? From Henry's point of view he knew from the minute he started boxing that he had the power to knock out similar sized boys with one punch, and while he was certainly taught how to get into a position to throw the punches, he wasn't learning anything different to moves taught to his contemporaries. Henry might then fall into the category of those who believe that 'one punch' concussive punchers are born.

As time moved on and it became clear from Bill Brown that Henry had a talent for the sport the whole family encouraged him any way they could. His sister Dinah, who Janet claims was a bit of a 'tomboy' used to go running with Henry round the nearby school, Danesmead, which they both attended. Eventually a makeshift hut was built between the Wharton's trailer and the end of the site because by this time Henry's appetite for training was almost insatiable. The hut was kitted out with a punch bag and other exercise equipment.

Henry, like his siblings, didn't have a regular school education until he reached the age to attend secondary school and by then he had trouble with reading and writing. His mother Janet was astounded in later years when he came across as being very articulate when interviewed on television, and she puts this down to him teaching himself to read through his obsession with comics. By 1985, when Henry was seventeen, the family gave up life on the road and moved into a house in Dove Street, York when a more regular lifestyle emerged for those who were still at home. Janet feels that both herself and the children didn't miss the travelling life that much, "How could you?" she says, "when you had hot and cold running water and be able to take a bath anytime you wanted?" Simple pleasures which they hadn't been accustomed to in their previous existence.

Sadly for the family, dad Billy and Janet split up with Billy continuing to live in the caravan on the site in Fulford. There is no avoiding the issue that the family patriarch liked a drink, and when under the influence he could be less than kind. On occasion, he would think it beneficial to hit Henry a slap with the back of his hand 'just to keep him alert to the possibility of being attacked unexpectedly!'. Billy had a difficult life, taking on physically hard work at any opportunity just to feed his large family, with the luxuries of modern life being totally alien to him. But regardless of his drinking, and the occasional back-hander, Henry still thought the world of him.

It's perhaps relevant to consider what effect Henry's lifestyle had on his boxing career. The manual labour all were expected to undertake from an early age would bring a natural level of strength and fitness. The excess fruit and vegetables available while working on the farms for most of the year ensured that a healthy diet was possible and with being part of such a large family by modern day standards there can be little doubt that everyone would have had to pull their weight. For some reason, travelling families have traditionally been involved in fighting,

or boxing, of some sort or another, and there was a clear
background of boxing within the Wharton family tree, with
grandfather Henry, father Billy, older brother Eddie, and in
later years, younger brother Alfred.

Once Henry's mother Janet had allowed him to attend the
York ABC, she became very supportive and enjoyed attending
his fights. That was until one evening before an ABA
qualification bout when she looked across the hall and saw the
height of Henry's opponent. "I thought to myself – what type
of mother am I? I'm sitting here about to watch my son getting
punched on the head. This isn't right." Nevertheless Henry's
amateur career was established and he was becoming a well
known name in local sport circles, featuring regularly in the
local press.

After about three years at York ABC, a situation presented
itself leading to a change of direction. For some time Henry had
become aware that his progression appeared to be stalling. He
didn't seem to be able to stop his opponents anymore. He
mentioned this to his dad who tried to explain it away by
suggesting that his body was growing in spurts leaving him
temporarily weakened, but that wasn't the full story. Without
wanting to seem big-headed, Henry explained that sparring in
the gym wasn't challenging him anymore. He was 'pulling' his
punches because he knew he could hurt his opponents, and they
were after all, his friends. This all came to a head at a show one
night when Henry fought a lad he'd beaten previously. He lost
on points and in addition, his trainer Bill Brown, due to work
commitments, couldn't be in his corner. This led to a review the
following week by all the coaches, Henry, and his dad. Bill

Brown, that wise old head, and being totally unselfish told Henry he had to move to another club if he hoped to continue his progress. Although reluctant to leave, the decision was made, and a new home had to be found.

CHAPTER 2

St Patrick's ABC

One night dad Billy told Henry to pack his bag and come with him. They walked to York railway station and took the train to Leeds. On the way Henry kept asking where they were going. This is how he recalled the events that night. "I swear we got off the train and remember the streets were core black. All the buildings were boarded up. Of course today they are all wine bars. We were walking down the street and I thought, 'where in the world are we going?'. We must have went into four pubs my dad used to go into, because we originally came from Leeds. I kept nudging him and saying, 'come on dad we've got to go to the club.' 'Don't you worry my lad, we'll go'. Anyway, four pubs later we walked into Bass St Patrick's boxing club and it would have been two and a half miles from the railway station. I still don't know to this day how my dad made the decision to take me there."

At the time the club was thriving having several internationalists and the man in charge, Terry O'Neill, was a very well respected coach having taken the English squad to the Commonwealth games in 1974. That first night the principal trainer O'Neill had taken boxers off to a show elsewhere and one of the boxers, Gary Atkin, had returned to the club on his own because he'd forgotten something. Atkin can place the date exactly, 2 December 1982, because it was the night of his last fight. Henry and his dad spoke to Atkin and asked him which nights the club was open. He was told that he would train on Monday, Wednesday and Friday nights. Henry queried what happened on the other nights and at the weekends, and Atkin explained that the club closed on a Sunday, but the seniors used it on Tuesday, Thursday and Saturday mornings. Gary had a smile to himself when the young Wharton declared that he'd attend EVERY night.

Terry O'Neill, with all his experience both at local and national level knew immediately he had found someone special. "When I first met him I took him by the shoulders to have a look at him and I could feel how solid and strong he was for a young lad, and when I watched him move about the ring I could see that he had a natural style, good balance. And could he punch!"

For the rest of his amateur career he attended at Bass St Patrick's every night, as promised! Not only did he train five nights a week but he developed a personal fixation which forced him to be the last boxer to leave the gym. Each night as the club was emptying Henry would be watching the clock and the remaining boxers hoping the others would stop soon, allowing him to catch the ten o'clock train back to York. On many occasion Atkin and O'Neill had to drive their young charge to the station themselves and often, having to catch a later train, Wharton would be struggling back home around midnight.

Henry's mother, Janet, can remember one such cold winter's night when her seventh child got back to the house. She had to prise his fingers from a bag because they were frozen stiff after the two mile walk back from York station.

Let's just pause for a moment to consider the practical

implications for the teenage Wharton. Coming from a family with ten siblings, living in cramped accommodation in the caravan, Henry would set out around 5pm and walk a couple of miles to York railway station. He would then travel around twenty five miles by train getting off at Leeds. He then had a further couple of miles to walk to the gym before embarking on a physically demanding training schedule including floor exercises, shadow boxing, punching a variety of bags, practicing techniques on hook and jab pads, ending with several rounds of sparring before returning home by the same route. This happened every night, every week for years and thankfully all the effort paid off handsomely.

St Patrick's gym was filled with top level amateur boxers, many of whom had represented their country, and the sparring was hard! Henry recalls. "When I went to Leeds I was sparring with people just a little bit older than me but they were wearing England vests. I used to leave the gym at times and think, 'God that was tough, really tough.' There was Tony Massey, David Binns, Mark McCreath and so on. They were all good talented boxers and it was tough on me. There were two or three guys at my weight and only one of us could enter some of the championships. Tony Massey was my weight, in fact we had to have a box-off at a show, to decide who'd go through."

Wharton didn't just absorb all the coaching he received in a passive way – he analysed everything in his own head. He was, and is, a boxing fan. In those days he read everything he could about boxing and would try to incorporate some of what he read into his own game. When he was getting caught with punches he used to work out why it was happening and try methods to avoid a repeat. At the next training night he would arrive with the intention of not receiving a particular punch, having worked on his defence in private. Likewise, if he was finding it difficult to land punches he would think it through and come up with potential solutions to try out the next night. Lessons learned in this way usually last longer because the individual has developed them himself.

Dad Billy, too, had a novel way of assisting his son in terms of his conditioning! One day he arrived at the camp site in York with a dilapidated looking car. He got Henry out of the caravan to show what he'd got him. Being aged around sixteen years at the time, Henry tried to explain to his dad that he was too young to drive. Billy replied," Don't be daft lad, you've to smash it up with this sledge hammer to build up your strength!" When the young Wharton had finished, the car resembled one of those you see crushed by machinery in the scrap merchants!

The 'car theme' was to be a continuing issue for young Wharton. As we know he was dedicated to his training, but that same 'drive' led him into deep waters. A year or so later, knowing he was going to miss his train to Leeds, Henry decided that he'd take a scrapped mini car which sat unused on the camp site. Things went smoothly – for a time. Henry did get to his routine training night, but it was on the road home when disaster struck. He was pulled over by the police who were suspicious on seeing a young lad driving a 'banger'. Of course the mini had no documentation at all and they couldn't find details of who owned it. Our rising 'star' was arrested and locked up at a police station in Leeds. Henry was oblivious to the rising concern when he failed to return to the caravan at the usual time. The family phoned Terry O'Neill and others who confirmed he'd been at the gym. Contact was made with local hospitals, but still no trace. Eventually a local detective, Mick Thompson, who helped out at St Patrick's, found Henry, got him bailed, and took him back to his house for the remainder of the night.

In October 1985, a few months short of Henry's eighteenth birthday, St Patrick's had organised an Anglo-Scottish group to go out to New Jersey in the States for a clash with an American select. On the day of the fights one of the American coaches approached Henry, being the youngest boxer there, and in an almost apologetic manner trained to explain that his (Henry's) trainer had 'done his best'. Not understanding what he was meaning, Henry sought clarification. The American coach explained that his original opponent had pulled out with a hand injury and his replacement was 'really good'.

The 'opponent' turned out to be Glenwood Brown. Brown turned professional a year later and would go on to win thirty four of his first thirty five fights, twenty four inside the distance. Brown challenged unsuccessfully for both the IBF and WBA world welterweight crowns before retiring in 2000.

Henry remembers the contest well. "It was a good fight. It was good while it lasted anyway, but he was too good for me. It was a cracking fight because I went for him, I always went for everybody. I really shook him up, and that was a wrong path, because I went for the finish. He had a head guard on, and I didn't. I had him going but then he hit me to the body, to the body, to the body, and I swear it didn't hurt. Because I was a novice at the time I let him keep hitting me to the body, and the accumulation of punches took its toll and the last punch was 'the straw that broke the camels back'. I was down and when I got up my corner man, Harry Hare, threw in the towel."

When Wharton got home there was a period of self examination. He'd never been beaten like that before, and being the dedicated young man he was, he wondered how he could rectify what he'd done wrong. However, it was Terry O'Neill who was to steer him in the right direction. O'Neill explained that his body was growing and that he simply couldn't make the welterweight limit anymore and that trying to keep his weight down was weakening him. After some argument from his determined young student, Henry had to accept that he should move up to light middleweight, and very quickly thereafter he could feel his strength returning.

A year later, the American fixture was reversed, this time with the match taking place in the Queens Hotel in Leeds. The New Jersey opponent for Wharton was Darrin Oliver, three years older than Henry, and reckoned to be a star performer. Henry can recall his thoughts on this fight. "This was not the same Henry Wharton anymore. I had built myself up, I think I might have been a light-middleweight, and I was much stronger. The fight set off and they thought they'd do the same result and he came like a bull in a china shop. Body shots, every shot in the book and I'll tell you, he hit me with most of them. He battered me from pillar to post, he really did. I sat back down, at the end of the second round, I think, and the coach was saying, 'move, move.' I said, 'I'm not going to move no more, I'm going to knock him out.' This was the last fight of the night, and I just knew I was going to knock him out. I had rallied a bit towards the end of the second round, and I could just feel something- he had given me enough of his punishment and I just felt I'd got him and they were going on in the corner,' no, no, keep your hands up', but I was as sure as anything I'd get him. I came out and beat him all over the ring, it was as if someone had switched a light on, and I had him down twice, and the last punch I hit him with he couldn't get back up and was counted out. I got a standing ovation that night, and still when I go to Leeds now, even though I've had all my professional career, people can still relate back to that show because they can't recall a comeback like that to this day." Even now Wharton retains the excitement and thrill he felt that night and gives the impression that he doesn't simply remember the occasion, but can actually feeling it. Oliver's amateur pedigree didn't carry him far within the professional ranks, losing most of his fights, and in fact lost in a round to future great, Bernard Hopkins.

Even in those young, early days as an amateur, Wharton had an inner belief that he was on a road to, as he says, 'somewhere'. He didn't know where that 'somewhere' was, but he was determined to get there and his commitment to training and learning were examples of a burning desire that was unquench-able. Nevertheless, there is one ingredient any aspiring boxer should have in their arsenal and that is experience. An experience which comes from dealing with adversity and fighting opponents who bring something new to the 'table'. Henry got this from fighting the likes of Brown and Oliver. Brown, at the time, was a much more accomplished boxer with a terrific body punch, and Oliver benefited from being a fully developed man, fighting in all sorts of tough venues on America's east coast. Henry absorbed everything from those fights like a sponge and they amounted to further 'ticks in the box' on the Wharton 'report card'.

Henry was now of an age to enter the ABA title trail, in effect the British amateur championships. These championships follow a regional route, from which qualifiers move forward to meet fellow area winners before reaching the finals, usually held in late spring, at Wembley. Wharton's first fight in the Yorkshire Division was on 29 January 1987 at Townville Working Men's Club in Castleford. His opponent was L Smith from Croft House ABC in Sheffield. Henry got off to flier beating Smith in the 1st round. Henry was due to fight the winner of the other fight at middleweight to decide the Yorkshire Division champion. M Holden from Mexborough won on points against D Hobson from Market District ABC, but he was unable to compete in the final, so Henry had a walkover.

The next stage was the North East Counties Semi-Finals on 12 February at Spa Royal Hall in Bridlington. Both opponents, for John (Cornelius)Carr from Grangetown ABC and Wharton, failed to appear, resulting in both getting a bye through to the Final.

The Final itself was held at Owton Manor Social Club in Hartlepool on 5 March. Nine days before the fight Wharton came down with chickenpox and recalls how he felt. "I had bumps all over and I never trained or nothing. A couple of days before the fight the doctor advised me not to box, but I decided to go for it. He moved all the time and boxed a clever fight." Carr won a close contest on points and progressed to the next round. He had an impressive run before losing in the ABA Final on points to Rod Douglas. From Middlesbrough, Carr would go on to have an excellent career as a professional winning thirty four of thirty eight fights. He turned pro in September that year winning twenty six of his first twenty seven contests, annexing the British Super Middleweight title on the way. He eventually fought and lost in an attempt at the WBO world Super Middleweight championship against Steve Collins and retired in 2001.

Despite the defeat from Carr, Wharton's amateur career was gathering pace and drawing attention far beyond his regional boundaries. Henry remembers travelling down to Luton to take on a top performer at the time, Keith Wallace from St Albans. His team knew that many of the England selectors were going to be present that night and it was a clear opportunity to impress. Impress he did, knocking out Wallace in the 3rd round.

After being invited to join the GB Olympic squad training in October, Henry's hopes were being raised, and he prayed for an opportunity to fight in a full international for England. Fighting for England was a major issue for Wharton and he used to spend hours daydreaming about it. Sometimes dreams do come true, and it certainly did for Henry. The Wharton family used to get there mail delivered to the local Post Office and when he went there on one occasion he received a letter advising him he was selected to fight against Poland. Once over the initial excitement he recalled an item he'd read in the Boxing News about a Polish boxer, Wieczorek, who had recently knocked out the top level German, Henry Maske, and wondered if he would be his opponent.

On 18 October in the northern Polish town of Slupsk, Bogdan Wieczorek was indeed the opposition. He'd finished third in the Polish championships, no mean feat given the status of amateur boxing in that country. The fight couldn't have worked out better for the York teenager. The Pole stormed out in the first to meet Wharton, which proved to be the wrong tactic, because Henry knocked him out with a left hook!

Three and a half weeks later, the Wharton star was still rising when he took on Ireland's Ray Close at the leisure centre in Bletchley. The bout was televised by the BBC and the resultant first round knockout victory brought the Yorkshire man's exploits to a wider audience. Henry recalled, "I trained really hard because of what everyone was saying about him. A big left hook, and a standing count brought about the end." Close would go on to have a very successful professional career. He won twenty five of twenty nine contests and along the way became European champion. He fought Chris Eubank to a draw in a bid for the WBO world title, losing on a split decision in a re-match.

However, the York express train was about to be derailed. His next international appearance was on 13 December in a match against Czechoslovakia in Prague. In the other corner would be Mikhail Franek. The Czech had been the world junior light middleweight champion two years previously a fact Henry was not aware of at the time. In England, before they set off, Henry discovered he was almost a stone over weight. Although aware that he could put on weight very easily, and as a result of being perhaps a bit too confident, he failed to control his eating. He can remember jogging in a sweat suit with fellow team member Neville Brown trying to get the excess off before leaving the country.

As Henry explained, "I'd had two bouts and won them in the

first round. I wasn't big headed but you get to think you can beat anybody. I wasn't training properly. I was eating a lot. I was nine pounds over, about a day and a half before the fight. By the actual morning I had lost five pounds and Kevin Hickey the national trainer couldn't believe how much I was still over the limit. I told him I had eaten and drank a lot that morning. He said we'd see how it came off. I trained in my own room in a sweat suit and ate nothing for the rest of that day. When I fought I was absolutely weak. I had no energy. My legs were trembling and I had no power at all."

In no condition to fight Wharton received three standing counts in the first round and was stopped by the referee. Even as a twenty year old Henry was an 'eternal optimist' with an endearingly positive nature and instead of dwelling on the defeat and the possible causes, he looked upon it as a valuable lesson and another building block towards a successful boxing future.

Young Wharton may well have taken this episode in his stride and shrugged it off, but it's likely that it had unforeseen consequences. The events in Prague, and beforehand, might have been the reasons why decisions were taken in the next few months which would tarnish his entire boxing career.

CHAPTER 3

Established Amateur

The circumstances surrounding the Franek disaster including bad eating habits, over confidence and a slackening in his previously vigorous training regime, were all dealt with immediately by the chastened St Patrick's boxer, and it was fortunate that he had an early opportunity to redeem himself just over a month later.

Clearly the England selectors were prepared to stick with him after the defeat from Franek and he was out again in his cherished 'England' vest at Gateshead Leisure Centre on 22 January. The match was against Scotland and his opponent was a tough Dumfries man, Jim Mair. Wharton was back on song and after a relatively even first round, the Englishman began to move forward confidently and spectators could see that the left hook was coming. When it landed Mair was badly shaken and eventually counted out.

It was not all work and no play for the star internationalist. Former professional boxer Ron Hopley who trained at St Patrick's had become firm friends with Henry. Hopley lived in Ripon but spent most weekends in York staying with the large Wharton family in Dove Street. To put it mildly, they had an active social life! The night would begin playing pool at a nearby pub, and being quite handy with the cues they earned themselves extra drinking money. They would then move into the centre of York, and with Henry and his family being well known they usually managed to get into the night clubs free of charge which meant more money for drinking. As typical young men they were intent on enjoying themselves, but perhaps inevitably there would be the occasional confrontation. Ron remembers one such time when Henry went off to the toilet and took longer than expected to return. Ron later discovered that while in a cubicle Henry became aware of someone banging repeatedly on the door. He has to be admitted that when he opened the door he was in a bit of a temper. One of the local rugby league players was standing. He pushed a false tooth out and warned Henry not to 'mess' with him. When Ron arrived the first rugby player was flat on his back and another had just received a 'Glasgow kiss'. Not the Marquis of Queensberry rules, but effective nevertheless.

There were girls of course, and they can get you into trouble as well. Ron and Henry had gone back to a girl's flat one night when they heard a loud banging at the door. On looking out they saw that a boyfriend had arrived and, being suspicious, was trying to put the door in with a shovel. As Henry climbed out a rear window to get round the front in an effort to placate the enraged partner, poor Ron was advised in the meantime to arm himself with a pool cue as the locks were about to give way. Fortunately for all concerned both 'likely lads' survived to fight another day.

Not surprisingly around this time Henry met his first serious girlfriend in the shape of local girl Anita Burkitt. Isaac Inns, fellow gypsy , and if we remember, a club mate of Henry at the York ABC, can recall clearly the night Henry first came across

Anita. It was at Isaac's brothers twentieth birthday celebration at Barnhams pub in the city. Soon after this they became an item but unfortunately for Anita, Henry's Saturday nights were sacrosanct as far as socialising with Ron and others were concerned.

Even though Ron and Henry might have had a skin full on a Saturday night they still found time for boxing. In the small basement of his mothers house they'd rigged up some lighting and on Sunday mornings out would come the gloves and Ron, Henry and occasionally Henry's older brother Eddie would go at it hammer and tongs with the stale alcohol oozing out their pores.

In early 1988 Henry had two massive motivational drivers which were firmly at the forefront of his mind – his next challenge for the ABA championship, and of greater significance, the chance of going to the Olympic games in Seoul. He'd proven he could punch at the very top level knocking out the representatives from Poland, Ireland and Scotland. On the domestic front he'd been knocking out opponents at every level for over seven years and had been considered good enough to train with the GB Olympic squad. He was becoming well known, and feared, within amateur boxing circles and his reputation went well beyond North Yorkshire.

So, the ABA trail started again on 3 February with the North East Counties (Humber and Yorkshire Divisions) qualifications at the Irish Centre in Leeds. The unfortunate first victim for the 'fired up' Wharton was Hull Fish Trades representative, Steve McMahon who unfortunately didn't hear the bell to end round one. In the Final later that night Mark Whitehouse from Tom

Hill Youth ABC lasted an extra round before he too succumbed. Henry himself can explain how his reputation as a big puncher, and his status as an England internationalist was making it difficult to get opponents to fight him. "His trainer said to him, 'your fighting Henry . . . . ', and he (Mark Whitehouse) said,' no I'm going to fight him!', and fair do's to him. I remember it well, I was shocked. In the changing room when they came back in and said,' he's taking the fight!' . I couldn't believe it. I didn't think I was better than anybody else but I was so used to fighters pulling out. He took the fight and I remember he was a tough boy, really tough, but I got to him in the end and I got him in the second, but it was tough while it lasted."

These victories moved Wharton on to the North East Finals held at Gateshead Leisure Centre, his second visit there in a couple of months. His opponent was to be Ian Meredith from Newbiggin Dolphin ABC, who himself had built a reputation as being a big puncher. Both boxers had now acquired a large fan base, and to avoid any prospect of rowdiness the bout was put on early in the evening before the drink started to flow. It was clear from the off that both boxers were intent on a quick finish and unfortunately for Ian, Henry landed a left hook in the first round and it was all over for the North East lad.

A month later, on 18 March at the same location, the Northern Counties Finals were held, and Henry's opponent was Eric Noi from the Fox ABC in Rochdale. The result of this bout is still a source of good humoured banter between the fighters some twenty five years later. In Henry's own words here's how he saw the bout. "I thought I clearly won the fight. Eric Noi's a good friend of mine and I like the guy, but we had a set too which puts you in good stead for the rest of your life. I knocked him down and I thought he was completely out cold. He got up at eight and he came at me like a man possessed and I still thought I won the fight. I said to him not so long back, 'me and you are big pals, pals for life, but I still won that fight!'.

The officials gave Noi the fight by a majority decision.

As we know this was Olympic year and the British selectors had the unenviable task of choosing who would go to Seoul. Wharton was clearly in the running because he'd been England's first choice at middleweight over the last year. He suspected that Welshman, Nicky Piper, was also being considered and didn't believe that Scotland had anyone in contention. Being totally honest, at the time, he felt certain that he'd be picked.

Henry had been training regularly with the Olympic squad, training alternative weeks with them and at home. He had even been kitted out with the squad tracksuit, which he still has to this day. Nevertheless, he wasn't selected, and he still can't understand why. Eight British boxers went to Seoul with the team being unrepresented in three weight categories, including middleweight. Wharton has never got over the disappointment he felt. In many ways it has tarnished what was an exceptionally successful amateur career, one in which he reckons he won 89 of 100 contests. He's not one for living in the past, and still retains an infectious enthusiasm for life, but he remains visibly upset at this episode, because he simply can't get his head around it.

The selectors chose only eight out of a potential eleven boxers, and there was at the time speculation the budget available to the selectors was insufficient to take a full squad, which in modern times is hard to comprehend given he range of funding streams available now. Henry had also failed to win the ABA title, but the eventual winner was also rejected. Perhaps his stunning defeat by the world class Czech, Franek, and his poor preparation was a deciding factor. Could the 'fall out' with the Scottish ABA early in the year have been an issue, and it may be worth noting that Scotland had three boxers in the team.

This setback didn't seem to effect Wharton's prospects greatly on the international scene, because in June he was on his travels again, this time to Athens for the Acropolis Cup. This was a demanding three day event in the soaring heat of Greece, with boxers from all over Europe, many of whom were putting finishing touches to their preparations for the Olympic Games. It was testament to the loyalty of his friends that Isaac Inns and four others from York followed Henry to Athens, having to scrape every penny they earned to make the long journey.

In the Quarter Final Wharton met the Danish representative, Peter Madsen, who he stopped in the first round. He'd a tougher battle in the Semi Final beating the Dutchman J Christianssen on points. This gave Henry the chance to watch the other Semi between the Italian boxer and the home favourite Giorgios Iaonnidis. Wharton was hoping and praying for the Italian to win because each time the Greek throw a punch the fans cheered to the rafters. This seemed to have the desired effect because the local boxer won on points although Henry felt the Italian deserved the decision. Iaonnidis went on to fight in the Olympics losing in the first round to a fighter from the Cameroon.

Henry knew he was up against it in the Final in more ways than one. This would be his third fight in three days and to continue to make the 75 kgs weight limit was difficult. He'd to train hard and watch his intake whenever he'd to make the weight for a competition or international. To do this on three days consecutively was not pleasant although sweating in the heat did help. In any case the Greek won the fight on points and when standing with the silver medal on the podium Wharton felt sick because he knew within himself that he'd been robbed.

Wharton tried to remain positive after the massive blow of missing out on the Olympics and in December he was back out in the England vest for an international against Ireland in Dublin. His opponent was a 6' 4" Kilkenny policeman, Gerry Lawlor. To this day Henry feels that this was the most awkward person he ever fought. Being a southpaw and so tall he simply couldn't reach him even though he chased him all over the ring. He did force two standing counts in the third and won the fight clearly even though the English judge gave it the Irishman??

With his great amateur ambition of fighting in the Olympics gone, the only remaining goal, having already represented his country on numerous occasions, was to win the ABA title before finally turning professional. His third attempt at the domestic honours began very quietly on 2 February 1989 with the Yorkshire Divisional stage at the Royal Hall in Harrogate. It couldn't have been more quieter because he had no opponent!

Aside from boxing however, Henry, had to earn a living outside the ring, and although he tried painting and decorating he was having difficulty making ends meet. The final straw came when his 'old banger' he used to travel back and forwards from York to Leeds eventually passed to the great 'car lot' in the sky. Appeals for sponsorship did not fall on deaf ears and it was testament to Wharton's growing popularity that local York firms AFG (Fulford), and the Bargain Centre on Bishopthorpe Road stepped in to help. In addition St Patrick's ABC in Leeds appealed for assistance and local businessman Bill Brennan donated £2,000.

Around this time Henry met a man who would become a life long friend, although he couldn't have expected it in the circumstances. Denzil Browne was another Leeds amateur who was gaining a reputation far outside his native city. At thirteen and a half stones he was a heavyweight in the unpaid ranks, although he'd later fight as a cruiserweight when he turned professional. He knew Wharton from seeing him at amateur tournaments. As they were both hoping to do well in the ABAs, Terry O'Neill and Browne's trainer Brian Rose arranged for them to spar each other at St Patrick's gym. When they were going to the sparring session Rose warned Browne to be on his guard because he knew Wharton's growing status as a hard puncher. Denzil himself remembered how he reacted to the advice. "I was a 'street kid' from a 'black' part of Leeds. I was winning my fights easily and I was thinking, 'there's no little white kid going to cause me problems.' Well, we started sparring and when he caught me with left hooks to the head my head was ringing. For days later my head was buzzing from the punches."

A month later, on 3 March, Wharton was back again at Gateshead Leisure Centre for the North East Counties Finals. In the opposite corner was Paul Hitch from the Horden and Peterlee club. Hitch was a good quality opponent but was stopped in the second round.

On 16 March at the Forum in Wythenshawe Henry met his

old nemesis Eric Noi in the Northern Counties Final. Noi had
been called into the England squad before this and he and Henry
had friendly banter about the forthcoming battle. In the end
Wharton won the fight, forcing Noi to take two standing counts
in the last round. Henry took even greater pleasure from the fact
that he'd beaten Noi on his own turf, but admits that it'd been
a really close fight and at one point could have gone either way.

The momentum was building and it was back to more
familiar ground for the ABA Quarter Finals because they were
held at Gateshead Leisure Centre. His opposition on 5 April,
Lee Woolcock, had a much longer journey than Henry to get
there having to travel all the way from Canvey Island. Although
Henry won, there'd been some controversy afterwards when the
Boxing News reporter gave the fight to Woolcock. At the time,
and now, Henry can't believe that anyone present could have
thought he'd lost. "I can't explain what that did to me. That was
stupid. Woolcock met me head on and I put him down in the
first round. After that I had trouble with my left hand. I'd caught
him on top of the head."

This was the first real occasion when Henry realised he'd a
problem with his hands. It's likely that Wharton suffered a
hairline fracture on the middle knuckle of the left hand and
indeed could actually separate the knuckle by forcing down on
it!

The championship was moving forward at great pace and
thirteen days later at King George's Hall in Blackburn Wharton
faced Jimmy Farrell from Channel View ABC in the Semi Final.
There was simply no stopping the 'in form' Wharton and two
left hooks won him the fight in the first round.

The crowning glory for Wharton's long amateur career was only one fight away, the ABA Final at Wembley on 5 May against Seymour Johnson from Gloucester. Johnson was a good boxer, but not a puncher having won all his fights on points. There was no doubt that the Yorkshire boxer was a massive favourite going into the fight.

Wharton knew that Johnson would be difficult because he was a southpaw and liked to box on the back foot, but he'd felt that Lee Woolcock had been the fighter to avoid and as he'd beaten him Henry was confident of winning the championship. As the first round progressed Wharton had retained his composure even though he hadn't been scoring as well as he'd hoped, but there was no sense of panic. As the round was drawing to a close Wharton could feel he was getting closer to landing the big punches and sensed he was finally getting to him. What happened next caused a huge tremor in the Wharton boxing career and it's as well to hear what the boxer had to say to try to understand it. "It was a stupid moment. I'd never done anything before with malicious intent. The heat of the moment got to me. I wanted to be national champion and I knew this was the last hurdle and I really wanted to win. Because I had just missed, I swear, it was like when the bell went, I thought to myself, 'I've got you.' I hit him, and I can't change it now. I punched him on the chest, and as I was doing it I knew it was wrong but I couldn't stop it. I knew I had infringed the rules. Terry never said anything in the corner, nor did I, but we both knew something would happen, and I'd lose the first round, but I still fancied myself to win. When I got up to start the next round I thought I'd get a public warning and that would be it but never in my life did I think I would be chucked out. I couldn't understand at first what was happening. The next few moments are still a blank to this day. All I could think about was that I hadn't won the title. What I'd done was a gesture to say to him, 'I've got you now.' The result changed my life because I knew then I was finished with amateur boxing."

At the time Wharton's army of fans almost caused a riot and it was Henry himself and his team who managed to calm the situation down. The general opinion from ringside was that the referee had been very harsh. Certainly a warning and a point deduction would have been in order but a disqualification, particularly in an ABA Final, was considered extreme. It has also to be remembered that the decision wasn't taken in the spur of the moment, the referee had a full minute to make up his mind. Henry struggles to explain why he did it, but we do see similar incidents on a regular basis on the sports field – a defender handling the ball in the box, or committing a wild tackle leading to a sending off at a crucial time in the game. They all happen in an instant, with no time to think, and in moments of heightened tension. For Henry, his actions that night, coupled with his failure to make the Olympics, cast two huge shadows over what had been an otherwise glittering amateur career.

Three days later Wharton was selected for the European Championships but was forced to withdraw, publicly at any rate, due to a chipped bone in his hand and the cracked knuckle. In truth though, he was still bitter at how the ABA Final had ended and there were no circumstances which could have persuaded him to attend. His days as an amateur had come to an end.

CHAPTER 4

Punching for Pay

The manner in which Henry lost the ABA final just confirmed in his own mind that his amateur days were over. Terry O'Neill had been approached by a number of potential managers who wanted the Wharton signature on a contract. On the night of the ABA finals, Mickey Duff had been entertaining friends from abroad and at a loss about where to take them he'd realised the event was on at Wembley. It's likely Henry was already on Duff's radar but that night Duff talked to O'Neill and extended an invitation to come to London on 10 May. They were guests at the Herol Graham / Mike McCallum WBA middleweight title fight at the Royal Albert Hall.

Henry and Terry had discussions beforehand and Henry made it clear he wanted £10,000 as a signing on fee with a weekly wage of around £300 per week. Both travelled along with Gary Atkin down to London where Duff put them up in the White House Hotel. After dinner, Duff took them to the Albert Hall and afterwards they visited the Grosvenor Casino near Russell Square. While Gary and Henry enjoyed themselves, Terry and Mickey Duff got down to business. Terry initially told Duff that Henry wanted £10,000 up front and the wily old manager stated that he'd never given any fighter 'up front' money before. O'Neill, perhaps with a degree of pre-planning, offered to put up £5,000 if Duff matched this figure, thereby making them joint managers. Duff agreed to this deal. When they got back to Yorkshire, Gary Atkin claims that Terry O'Neill asked him if he wanted to take a quarter share for £2,500, but Gary, being surprised at the offer, and not familiar with the business, declined. So O'Neill sent off a cheque to Mickey Duff and a couple of weeks later Terry and Henry travelled to London for a press conference, again at the Grosvenor Casino, when contracts were signed for the benefit of the press. Duff also presented his new heavyweight, Henry Akinwande, to the photographers. Henry later went to Duff's offices in Wardour Street where he received his cheque and an advance on his weekly wages.

The summer months were now all about preparing for a professional career, and sensibly, Duff had agreed that Wharton would train in their amateur gym in Leeds. Trainer, Terry O'Neill, perhaps with a degree of sadness, took out a professional trainers licence, and left the amateur code for the time being. Although Henry was in reality receiving a weekly wage, albeit paid in advance, he did take on small painting and decorating jobs to keep the money coming in. In fact he would take on any work outwith his training schedule to augment his income whether it was roofing or other labouring work with relatives.

The first fight was arranged for early September and with that in mind Duff brought Henry down to train for a short period at Terry Lawless's gym at Canning Town in London. Wharton, surprisingly for his debut, was joint top billing at the 1,100 capacity Royal Hall in affluent Harrogate. On Thursday 21 September in a show promoted jointly by Duff and Lawless his professional career got under way. With over £5,000 worth of tickets sold by Henry alone, more than half those in attendance were supporting the local lad. Duff arrived in Yorkshire at the beginning of the week and began beating the drum for his new star, as only he knew how. There were interviews with the local and national press, photo shoots and announcements that Duff was seeking a bigger hall in Yorkshire for future fights, given the huge demand for tickets to see Wharton in action.

The scheduled first opponent had been Marty Duke, from Great Yarmouth, who'd four wins from nine fights, and probably a suitable fighter for Henry to face at this stage. As fight time approached Duke pulled out and was replaced by Birmingham's Dean Murray. Murray was twenty three years of age and won only four of nineteen contests. Then and now, young prospects, who have attracted significant financial outlay, tend to be protected in the early part of their careers, with the intention of easing them into the professional game and at the same time building a strong fan base. Without being unkind to Murray, he had no chance of beating, or even going the distance with Wharton but he would have been offered, and would have accepted, decent money for taking on the challenge.

In front of Wharton's massive support, many of whom were from the travelling community, Murray entered the lion's den hitting the scales at either 11st 8lb, or 12st 4lb, depending on whose version of the weigh in was to be believed. There was no doubt that Wharton weighed 11st 12lb, and local man, Mickey Vann, refereed. One hundred and nine seconds into the fight, Murray had been down four times before Mr Vann called a halt to proceedings with Murray commenting afterwards that he thought he'd been kicked by a carthorse. A beaming Duff told waiting reporters that he would have Henry back out at Wembley on 25 October on the undercard of Herol Graham's British title defence against Rod Douglas. Murray did not benefit greatly from this experience and had one more fight before calling it a day. Henry remembered the night well. "I had never been as nervous before a fight, then or since. I was in a right state. There was so much expected of me, and there had been such a build up that it had got to me. I wasn't used to such press interest and photographers and interviews. That's why I came out traps so quickly. I should have taken my time and got a bit of experience but I just came out and let go."

While Henry was preparing for his Wembley debut, Mickey Duff knew he had a TV date for 5 December and had set Terry O'Neill the task of finding a suitable venue in North Yorkshire to accommodate at least 1,500 spectators. Duff and Lawless were keen on providing an atmospheric setting for the TV producers and knew Wharton's fans would pack out any hall they found.

For the Wembley fixture Henry thought he'd be fighting the Austrian Sinisa Popovich but once again the original plan fell through. Duff's matchmaker Paddy Byrne's skills were being put to the test in terms of managing Henry's early career. Other British managers and their charges knew that Henry was a vicious puncher and was being groomed for stardom. Quite rightly their view was that if they were taking a fight in which there was a potential for a clean knockout defeat or at least a severe pummelling then they expected to be well paid for their trouble. Duff then had to balance the need to find a suitable opponent and how much that opponent would cost, with what he was prepared to pay. This is probably why an Austrian boxer was the preferred choice, but when this deal collapsed Byrne quickly found Welsh light heavyweight Kevin Roper prepared to fill the vacancy. This decision almost led to a calamity on fight night.

Henry had sold two hundred tickets to his fans who travelled over two hundred miles to London from North Yorkshire to see the local lad take on his second opponent. He himself had been training flat out and was keen to impress the London fight crowd and justify the enthusiasm Mickey Duff had shown for his fledgling career. The weigh in was at the Odeon cinema in Leicester Square and Wharton hit the scales at 12st. Later that night when Henry was in the arena and watching the fans starting to roll up, he began to get early notice that Roper was refusing to fight. The Welshman was quoted as saying that despite getting a purse of £1,500 he didn't want to box adding, "I don't want to be knocked out, it's as simple as that!" Matchmaker Byrne may have been furious, but Henry was shattered. All the pent up energy evaporated and he couldn't begin to imagine the reaction of all his Yorkshire friends and relatives when they got the news. He knew that money was tight for the majority of them and his sense of frustration was palpable.

Happily, however, Paddy Byrne worked his magic and from somewhere he found an opponent. Who knows today how this came about? Was cruiser weight Mike Aubrey in the crowd that night as a spectator, or had he been at home when the phone call from Byrne was made? Either way, the brave man got himself stripped and ready to face an emotional Wharton who was trying to pick himself up from the pits of despair. Aubrey had weighed thirteen and a half stone seven months previously and had won half of his dozen fights. When the ring announcer read out his weight as 12st 6lb there were howls of laughter from ringside, because he must have been at least two stones heavier!

Under these difficult circumstances Henry fought reasonably well scoring freely with hooks in the first, third and fourth rounds but was getting caught with long jabs in the second and took a stunning hook from the bigger man at the end of the fifth. Henry won on points, four rounds to two, and said afterwards, "I didn't find his extra weight a problem really, the extra reach was the worst bit."

Although Duff and his Yorkshire contacts had scoured the region for a larger venue for the December TV date, they'd to settle for Dewsbury Sports Centre, some forty miles from York, but only around ten from Leeds. In the meantime, Henry was becoming a bit of a celebrity in his home town and on the night before his third fight he was invited to switch on the Christmas lights at the York Evening Press's new premises on Walmgate.

Although York had a strategically significant role in the history of the country, and had a range of easily recognisable landmarks making it a centre for tourism, for some reason the contemporary population had little in the way of sporting success to enthuse over. Its football club generally languished in the lower leagues and horse racing at the city racecourse probably attracted the greatest interest. The emergence of a genuine local sporting hero had certainly stirred the city and Henry was becoming well known about town.

On 5 December, in front of the television cameras, Wharton stepped through the ropes to face American import, Ron Malek. The choice of opponent once again demonstrated the difficulties Duff was having in selecting a suitable foe, one who was willing to face the heavy punching newcomer and was prepared to accept a realistic fee for the privilege. Moreover, with the TV executives watching closely, Duff had to find someone worthy of the large audience sitting at home. The Wichita man seemed to fit the bill. He'd won half his twenty six fights and stopped eight of them. A couple of months previously he'd his first visit to Britain where he took Chris Eubank five rounds before being stopped. Wharton's purse for the Malek fight was £1,250 (£2,635 in 2013).

Given Duff's earlier problems in October with the late withdrawal of Kevin Roper, perhaps we shouldn't have been too surprised to learn that when Malek arrived at Heathrow, he couldn't catch a connecting flight to Leeds-Bradford Airport because London was fogbound. With the panic rising, Malek was billeted at a hotel in London before travelling by rail to Leeds where he immediately set about working up a sweat in a local gym. At the subsequent weigh in Wharton hit the scales at a remarkably light 11st 8lb, with the visitor two pounds less.

Henry was perhaps not as nervous, or as anxious to get started, as he was for his first fight with Dean Murray, but no one would have known, because three powerful left hooks had Malek down and out within an incredible twenty three seconds! This act of destruction had unexpected consequences, because soon after the British Boxing Board of Control contacted Mickey Duff and advised him they would be closely monitoring the standard of his future opponents. Henry however couldn't understand the fuss made by the Board and queried why they were watching him in particular when other more experienced fighters were 'knocking over' opponents with greater regularity.

The Board's warning had an immediate impact when they refused to allow Mustapha 'Eric' Cole to fight Wharton in early January believing he 'wasn't good enough'. It's worth looking at the background to this decision. Cole had taken part in ten fights up until then. Having won his first four he'd then gone on a six fight losing sequence. In the previous eleven months he'd visited Britain from his home in Ohio on three occasions. In February, he'd been stopped in five rounds by a very capable home fighter, Johnny Melfah. A month later he was stopped in the second by the brutal punching Rod Douglas, and on the same night Wharton fought Aubrey, Cole had been stopped in the fifth by Viktor Egorov, who was having his second contest. Was Cole then unsuitable for Wharton at this stage in his career? In his next fight Cole fought to a four round draw but lost his remaining twenty fights, fourteen inside the distance.

Regardless of the disquiet in the Wharton camp, a new opponent had to be found, and this was in the shape of Guillermo Chavez from Mexico. Chavez had won fourteen of seventeen fights, and in his last outing lost a battle for his national light heavyweight title.

Maybe Wharton had a point to prove to the Board when he entered the ring in Dewsbury on 11 January. If he was able to destroy a fighter they actually approved of in quick time, then would it not infer that it was not so much the quality of the opposition but simply that he punched so heavily. Wharton came in at 11st 11lb with the Mexican two pounds lighter, and local man Mickey Vann again refereed. As soon as the fight started Henry swung a left hook knocking Chavez into the ropes. He didn't fold however and came back swinging. A left to the body from Wharton brought the visitors arms down and a left and right had him on his back to be counted out by Vann after two minutes and forty six seconds. Although delighted at having proved a point, it was not all good news.

Wharton had suffered from a problem with the middle knuckle of his left hand since he'd damaged it originally when he beat Lee Woolcock in the ABAs almost a year previously. He hurt it again in the Chavez fight, and after visiting the Bradford orthopaedic surgeon, Arkos Nevelos, he'd to undergo laser treatment in an attempt to remove excess tissue. This put paid to a scheduled fight in Sunderland on the undercard of a Billy Hardy world title challenge.

Henry had by now moved out of the family home into a flat in Leeds allowing him to be nearer the gym, so that he could train twice a day. His training however was reduced to running and exercising without being able to punch anything solid due to the injured left hand. This resulted in his longest absence from the ring since his first fight, and his next outing took him back to Wembley on 3 March. As the hand healed, Wharton enjoyed the very best of sparring with fellow gym members, Tom Collins (who at the time had been British and European light heavyweight champion and recently fought for the world title), Denzil Browne (a cruiserweight who would fight for the British and Commonwealth crowns), Michael Gale (who would fight for the Commonwealth light heavyweight title), and both Nick

Manners (who would retire as the undefeated Central Area
Light heavyweight champion), and his brother, middleweight,
Colin.

Duff had managed to find a reasonably competent opponent
in the shape of Kentuckian, Joe Potts, who'd won four of his
seven contests and never been stopped. Worryingly however was
the fact that he was really a light middleweight although he did
weigh 11st 4lb for this match, over half a stone lighter than
Wharton. Once again there was a large following from Yorkshire
and Wharton began the fight in a confident mood, and seemed
a bit more composed. Unusually, it was a right hand which did
the damage, dropping Potts towards the end of the first round,
and he just beat the count. Potts got on his bike in the next
round with Wharton doing the chasing. Eventually a
combination put the visitor down again. The end seemed close
when a right to the body floored Potts, but as he struggled to his
feet the timekeeper rang the bell to end the round – a minute
too early!

Henry seemed to lose his way in the third, and the early part
of the fourth, with Potts becoming the aggressor, as his
confidence rose. The neutral observer would have been forgiven
for starting to doubt all the rave notices Wharton had been
getting, believing it might be possible that when the big punch
didn't succeed he might find himself in deep water. Wharton
seemed to answer that question, for the time being at any rate,
when another straight right hand dropped the American for the
count.

On paper it looked like another impressive win but there
were issues behind the scenes causing a bit of concern. The lack

of fire in the third, and most of the fourth, as well as some of Wharton's antics upset Terry O'Neill. During the fight, for some inexplicable reason, Henry would throw his right arm straight out from his side as if he was shaking it off, and then throw a punch. The commentator on TV, Harry Carpenter, thought he'd been trying to get some feeling into his injured hand, but O'Neill pointed out that it was the other fist that was injured adding, "I think Henry's been watching Sugar Ray Leonard. He does it in the gym and I've told him to cut it out. He was trying to open him up a bit. He was teasing Potts but I don't really approve. I suppose if it works then you can't complain, but I don't want Henry to get over confident and forget the basics. He's a fighter."

Wharton's famed left hand had never really healed, and it was constantly causing him pain. With Duff determined to have him fighting regularly, Henry didn't get a break from his strict training regime and it's easy to understand why, with the persistent punching of the bags and sparring, the injured hand didn't improve. No one in the camp could have realised then how this would eventually take its toll.

Another crowd of over 1,000 turned up on 11 April at the Dewsbury Sports Centre to see Henry face the experienced Mexican, Juan Elizondo. Elizondo had started out as a lightweight in 1972 and from fifty six fights had won twenty five and drawn three. In his only visit to Britain three years previously he'd been stopped in the second round by Tony Sibson. Wharton weighed 11st 12lb and officially the Mexican was listed as being three pounds heavier. Everyone must have realised that someone was having a laugh, because Elizondo was fat and out of condition. He'd have been struggling to get inside the cruiserweight limit.

The Mexican knew his way round a boxing ring, however, and could protect himself. Disaster struck in the very first round when Henry landed a solid left hand and he knew immediately that 'something had gone'. There wasn't too much pain, just a feeling of numbness and the knowledge that if he threw it again the damage would get worse. Wharton forced a stoppage in the third round, but there was little celebration in the corner. They all knew there was a problem. In the dressing room, when they took the gloves and bandages off, the left hand was badly swollen. Henry remembered that he felt "dead inside – I was gone". There's a photograph of Henry sitting in a corridor of Dewsbury Hospital awaiting the result of an x-ray, and it painted a desolate figure. A bone in his hand had been shattered, and at that point there were real concern that his boxing career might be over.

Mickey Duff wasted no time. He got Wharton on a train to London and the very next morning he'd a private consultation with a specialist at the Royal Free Hospital. It was only at this meeting that the gloom which had engulfed Henry began to lift. The surgeon, Richard Rushman, was able to assure him that not only could the hand be repaired, but that it would actually be stronger once it'd healed. Henry was operated on that night and a plate and pin were inserted to help the bones knit.

There then followed a series of monthly visits to the surgeon to monitor progress, and in the meantime a very frustrated Wharton did what he could to keep in shape. This was usually limited to running, and doing what he could in the gym while nursing a heavily bandaged hand. The monotony was partially broken with a holiday to Greece, and with boredom settling in due to an inability to train properly, Henry moved back in with his mother.

On one of the visits to London Henry got the good news that the bandage could come off, and he could start doing some very light punching on the bags. However there was a shock waiting for him just round the corner. When he went to London in July expecting the surgeon to give him the 'all clear', he was told that the plate and pin still had to come out. Henry virtually fainted on the spot, he couldn't understand why they had to be removed. He thought they were the reason why the hand would be so strong in the future. The surgeon explained that if Henry landed a very heavy punch, the strength and rigidity of the metal plate could shatter the surrounding bones, in fact the surgeon said his hand would 'explode'. So yet another operation was required on 31 July, and a further delay in resuming full time training. But, patience is a virtue as they say, and gradually Henry got the confidence back in his hand, and as the pain and discomfort disappeared he began once again to put his mind to progressing his career.

1: Early days on camp site with friends.
2: Henry with his first trainer at York ABC, Bill Brown.

This page: 3: A young Wharton proudly showing off his England vest. *Facing page: 4:* Henry with his buddy, Ron Hopley. *5:* 11 April 1990. A worried man about to have his broken left hand examined.

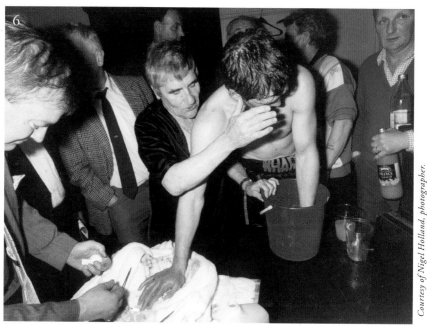

Courtesy of Nigel Holland, photographer.

Courtesy of Nigel Holland, photographer.

This page: 6: Terry O'Neill tries to cover Henry's eyes as the doctor stitches his hand after the Rod Carr fight. *7:* Dennie Mancini, Terry O'Neill, Mickey Duff, Henry and Gary Atkin. *Facing page: 8:* Henry with Gordon Strachan, then with Leeds United, before British title fight with Fidel Smith. *9:* Action from the Benn fight.

8

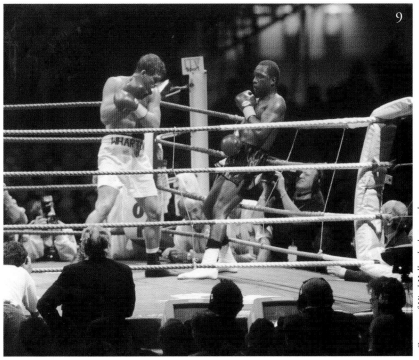

9

Courtesy of Nigel Holland, photographer.

Courtesy of Nigel Holland, photographer.

10: Press conference after the Benn fight. *11:* At Rocky's Bar training gym, Henry, Michael Gale, Gary Atkin, Denzil Browne and Ron Hopley. *Facing page: 12:* Terry O'Neill, Henry and dad, Billy. *13:* The Author with Henry and Gary Atkin.

14: Posing for the camera. Henry and Gary Atkin.

CHAPTER 5

Commonwealth Champion

Although Wharton was fighting fit again, and his hand seemed to be holding up while sparring in the gym, no one, and most importantly Henry, could know for sure what would happen when he landed a full bloodied shot on an opponents head or elbows. The importance of protecting his hands at training was not lost on Wharton. Henry could take upwards of twenty five minutes to wrap his hands up before training and he'd designed makeshift pieces of rubber to lie across his knuckles to take the pressure off. But, of course, this wouldn't be allowed when he was preparing for a proper bout.

His first fight back was on Thursday 18 October 1990 at Dewsbury Sports Centre against Chuck Edwards from Daytona Beach in Florida. Edwards had won seven of nine fights, with only one of those defeats inside the distance. In the build up Duff was telling the press that once Henry had proven his hand had mended, he'd be fighting every month until the end of the year. A new satellite broadcasting company called Sportscast, created by British Aerospace, were going to show the fight at pubs and clubs in Yorkshire owned by Cameron's the Brewers.

On fight night, experienced 'jack of all trades', Dennie Mancini, who was becoming a fixture, was again in Henry's corner and it was the wily old fight figure who took on the task of bandaging his suspect hands before the gloves went on. This became a routine for almost the full duration of Henry's career. Wharton had, and still has, the greatest affection for the sadly now deceased Londoner. He warmed to Mancini and felt that Dennie genuinely cared for his fighters, giving the impression that it was far more than a simple business arrangement. In later years it was Dennie who Wharton relied on in the corner to tell him the truth about how a fight was progressing and whether he was in front or not. Henry told Mancini at the very start of their relationship that if he felt he was falling behind and needed to put the foot down during a contest, regardless of what everyone else was shouting, he was to quietly whisper in his ear, "you need to go." In other words Henry would trust his judgement above most of the others.

Mancini's advice was not needed that night though, because the fight was over in sixty nine seconds. Edwards was down early on, and when he dropped the second time, referee Mickey Vann dispensed with the rest of the count. Half of the Australian Rugby League team had just settled down to enjoy the fight and it was over before they had a chance to draw breath. Afterwards Henry commented, "I caught him with a hard punch right on the elbow with the very first punch and I didn't feel a thing. That was beautiful, I knew then that the hand was stronger than ever. He dropped his hand so I went in." Caught up in the euphoria Henry continued, "I don't know what Mickey Duff thinks, because it's all down to him, but my feeling is that if I could take the twelve stones title then I could step down to middleweight easily and challenge someone like Benn or Herol Graham. That would be a fight everyone wants to see, the public would demand it. I'm quite confident I could handle a title fight soon, either British or Commonwealth."

Duff was true to his word with regard to Henry fighting regularly, and he was back out thirteen days later at Wembley against Dino Stewart from Muncie in Indiana. Stewart was really a light heavyweight with eight wins from fifteen fights and only one stoppage defeat. After this fight Stewart would win five in a row, taking on Iran Barkley at cruiserweight before bringing down his career up at heavyweight. This was a real step up in class, and if Henry didn't realise that, there was a further shock for him at the weigh-in. "I was sitting in the lobby sipping orange juice because I had to make a specific weight," remembers Henry, "when someone pointed out my opponent. I said 'that can't be who I'm fighting, he's six foot three. He's built like a giant. Why do I have to make this weight?' Anyway, at the weigh in the scales were raised up so the press could see, but of course, no one else could see the actual figures on the scales. I walked up the three or four steps and weighed in at twelve stones, one pound. He then walks up the steps and people get a different perspective when you're looking up and I remember thinking he simply can't be my opponent. He was announced as weighing twelve stones seven pounds. He was a lot heavier than that. He would have been well over thirteen stones – well over!'.

The show was televised by the BBC and top billing was Paul Hodkinson's defence of the European title, but because that ended early the Wharton fight was shown in its entirety. It turned out to be a close eight rounder with Wharton winning by a single session. He'd Stewart down in the seventh but looked lethargic at times and seemed to run out of ideas. It would've been easy for the onlooker to think that if Wharton couldn't knock them out early then he had no Plan B. However the real reason for the less than exciting performance soon came to light. "I hit him in the third round and I felt my right hand go instantly. Although my main punch was the left I needed my right hand to set them up and I couldn't throw it properly. I couldn't get any venom in the left because I was off balance. The fact that I knew the hand was gone didn't effect how I felt because I just thought about winning, winning ,winning. I didn't say much in the corner because they might have pulled me out. It wasn't painful but you simply couldn't throw it, I couldn't make a proper fist of it. It's unbelievable how one bone can make your entire hand and arm useless. I would never pull out, if they'd said in the corner they were pulling me out I wouldn't let them. In the seventh I hit him on the top of the head with a left and threw everything at him, including the right and I thought the ref should have saved him. He was as strong as bull, he just wouldn't go down. I told my corner at the end of the fight my hand was broken and they couldn't even take the glove off in the ring. As soon as the bell went the pain started and when they tried to take the glove off I had to tell them to stop. They had to cut the glove off in the dressing room and I stayed in London that night and went to Mr Rushman the next day. My world had fallen apart, I thought I was finished."

Further surgery followed resulting in more delays to his career, but again the surgeon assured Henry his hand would heal and his spirits were uplifted when he won a poll of Boxing News readers nominating him as the Prospect of the Year for 1991.

Wharton re-commenced sparring at the beginning of March

and the quality within his own gym couldn't have been better. Again there were Colin and Nick Manners, Tony Massey, Tom Collins on occasion, Michael Gale and Ron Hopley. He was scheduled to fight again at Dewsbury Sports Centre on the twenty first of the month, and his original opponent, Roy Bedwell pulled out- thankfully. He lost his next forty two fights in a row, twenty five by knockout! In came Mexican Francisco Lara who was now based in Switzerland. He'd fought for the Mexican title the previous year and had seventeen wins from twenty five fights. The Lara fight was another which ended early with referee Mickey Vann counting out the visitor towards the end of the first round. Behind the scenes Mickey Duff had put in a purse bid for Henry to challenge Londoner James Cook for the European title but history showed that this came to nothing.

Wharton's next fight was due on 9 May, for the first time at the atmospheric Leeds Town Hall, a venue which looked more like the inside of a cathedral. The fact is that Wharton could have packed out the venue with his own support, without any others on the bill selling tickets to friends and family. In St Patrick's gym there were a host of top quality professional boxers all roughly the same weight as Henry. They too, were winning fights and impressing the pundits. When you get good quality boxers in a gym, sparring every day with each other, tensions can arise. A problem was brewing within the gym in that Nick Manners, whose professional career had got off to a promising start, was starting to question why Henry seemed to be always topping the bill, meaning of course that he was earning bigger purses for the privilege.

This started off as being relatively light hearted banter with

Henry arguing that his opponents were of a higher standard. However, it was festering with both men and it reached its inevitable conclusion. Henry was sparring Nick's brother Colin one day, when he caught him with a heavy blow on the ropes. Colin lost his temper, as did Nick, who jumped over the ropes. Both then made for Wharton, with diminutive trainer Terry O'Neill trying to intervene. Meanwhile Henry too had lost the rag and was trying to tear his gloves off with his teeth so he could get at the Manners brothers. Finally, with the help of others in the gym, sanity prevailed and things settled down. The gym sessions carried on well into the future as if nothing had happened. There were no hard feelings.

Wharton's opponent in Leeds was to be Frank Minton from Indianapolis, yet another step up in class, and an ideal tester. The original choice had been another top level American, Sanderline Williams. Minton had mixed in the light heavyweight division but had been stopped by Iran Barkley, Christophe Tiozzo and Virgil Hill, and in his last fight been halted in four rounds by Mike McCallum. Terry O'Neill managed to get video copies of some of Minton's previous contests and knew he was a wily old pro who would give Wharton a tough fight.

Leeds Town Hall was packed to capacity with around 2,000 spectators. Although the majority in attendance were Wharton fans, the big fight of the night was the world light heavyweight contest between Tom Collins and Leonzer Barber. Henry got off to a quick start dropping Minton near the end of the first round. Thereafter the American seemed to catch Wharton quite easily but after forty one seconds of the seventh, a stunning left hook to the body brought another conclusive victory for the rising star. An unusual incident happened at the end of the sixth. There seemed to have been panic in Minton's corner and many thought he was going to retire but afterwards it transpired that he'd actually been choking on the water he was given! Afterwards Henry told the local press, "He was so experienced, he threw feints before he jabbed and it caught me nearly every time but that's something I've learned. This guy had all the experience and I just lapped it up. I've learned plenty. He's been in with the best and now people can't say its all hype."

Before the fight Mickey Duff had been claiming he'd arranged a fight with Australian Lou Cafaro for the vacant Commonwealth title, and soon afterwards, when Cafaro gave it up, Duff organised a battle for the vacant crown, coincidentally against another Australian, Rod Carr.

Carr wasn't particularly well known outwith the hard core boxing fan. He was from Melbourne and had won eleven of sixteen fights, drawing two, but nine of those wins had come by way of a knockout. He was coming down in weight from light-heavy and previously held the Commonwealth title, beating Ray Acquaye in October 1989. He'd lost his first defence to Cafaro.

Fighting for a title meant so much to Wharton. He can recall exactly what this chance meant to him. "When it was announced I was to box for the Commonwealth championship it was unbelievable for me because I always wanted to get myself in a position that I could fight for a title. That was all my life was about – titles. To be put on a pedestal. I thought – to be a champion, to fight even for a Central area title, I swear would have been good enough for me. But to fight for a Commonwealth title after ten fights was unbelievable for me and I trained really, really hard and I sparred every day, sometimes twice a day. I made sure I was prepared and I knew he'd be fit, and thank God I was fit. I had a tape of him when he boxed in America and he was winning the fight until he got stopped on a cut. I just knew this was going to be my toughest fight." Terry O'Neill had brought in additional sparring partners, much bigger men, including Glazz Campbell and Denzil Browne.

When the Australian group arrived in the UK, Carr's manager Keith Ellis immediately set about trying to get under Wharton's skin, but Henry refused to be drawn in. To be honest the fight didn't need any of that. On 27 June Leeds Town Hall was again filled to capacity and with supporters so close to the ring, and many positioned on the stage looking down, it would have been easy for the boxers to imagine they were entering the coliseum.

Carr's record, on paper at any rate, did him no favours. He turned out to be a very underrated boxer, fit, tough, physically strong and aggressive, with a left jab which would land repeatedly on Wharton's face like a piston. The Aussie's team had done their homework on Henry and knew he didn't like to fight on the retreat. With the jab landing constantly Wharton couldn't get set to land his big punches and everybody knew he was in for a tough night. However, in the second round, it looked like Henry's big punch might just shorten things a little. Out of the blue Wharton landed cleanly for the first time and Carr didn't know what hit him. A further blow knocked him clean out of the ring. When this happens the stricken boxer is allowed twenty seconds to get back and onto his feet, bravely Carr made it just in time.

Referee Dave Parris had a strange experience in the next round. "I looked down at my shirt and it was splattered with blood. The next time I broke up the boxers I glanced at both their faces to see who was cut, but none of them were. The fight continued and there was blood splashing all over the canvas and I still couldn't see who was bleeding. At one point I thought somehow that I'd cut myself. Near the end of the round I saw blood dripping from Wharton's right hand. When the bell rang I went to his corner and saw that the blood was coming from his hand."

Henry's corner saw that the glove was torn and the fight was held up for around three minutes while a new glove was found. By now Carr was fully recovered and he kept coming forward. His jab was a perfect punch and it was giving Wharton serious problems. In the seventh Henry landed again, this time with a body shot, and Carr went down. It looked to be all over, so much so, that one of Henry's fans, Georgie Harker, jumped into the ring to celebrate. But Carr wasn't going to give up that easy and he came storming back. At the end of twelve close rounds referee Parris, the sole judge, gave the title to Wharton by 118-117. With the way fights were scored in Britain in those days, this may have equated to the referee giving Wharton six rounds, Carr four, with two scored a draw.

What may be surprising is that Henry firmly believes that this was the hardest fight of his entire career. He can recall vividly how he felt. "I don't know how I came through it. There

were times in that fight I didn't think it was possible to go on.
When I sat down on the stool, with things that happened and
the blood I lost, I was cold in the corner. From the shock. I swear
on my life towards the end of the fight that I didn't think I could
get back up. I don't know to this day how I did it. All these years
later I can still relate to how I felt then, and it gives me a tingle,
that's how bad I felt."

Once back in the dressing room, and the excitement
beginning to fade, Wharton realised how painful his right hand
was. Gary Atkin can recall that the right glove was saturated in
blood and that it dropped into a pail like a wet sponge. The
bandages were soaked in blood and when these were cut off
Henry had a lengthy cut on the back of the hand, just behind
the knuckles. This subsequently required five stitches to close
it. It would seem that, following discussions with Carr's team
later that night, Henry's right hand had split Carr's gum shield
and his teeth had gone right through the glove and protective
bandages.

There was also other damage to Henry's right hand, a fact that
he deliberately hid from O'Neill and Atkin. He noticed that the
first knuckle on his right hand had been pushed backwards and
the bone behind it had been broken. He made up his mind he
wasn't going to tell anyone because he suspected they'd make him
have another operation and that might have led to him being
stripped of his newly won championship. Neither of his corner
men knew this even up to the point that this book was being
prepared. The troubles continued in the days following the fight
when infection set in and he had to have penicillin injections.

Perhaps surprisingly for those who are not closely involved

in the boxing game, everyone headed back to St Patrick's gym for an 'after fight' party, including the Australians. Henry however was ill, and although he went along he has never forgotten how he felt. "We went back to Bass St Patrick's club and I had a pint of Guinness. I can still remember it, I thought I was going to die. I drank half a pint of Guinness and I don't know if I lost too much blood or I was dehydrated but I really thought I was going to die. I felt so bad. When I got home that night I got up about three o'clock in the morning and I ran my hand under hot and cold water and the pain was unbelievable. It wasn't where the stitches were it was at the knuckle."

When boxing people discuss the top middleweights and super middleweights from that era the usual names will be trotted out. It is highly unlikely that Rod Carr's name will be mentioned. The Australian was one excellent fighter. It's hard to find any fault in his make-up. He knew the game inside out. For any youngster setting out on a boxing career they would be well advised to seek out examples of Carr's fights and study how he threw the left jab. When it landed Carr's chin was tucked in tightly behind his shoulder with his right hand covering the entire right side of his head and it was thrown with so much venom that it would have given any fighter in history real problems. Having been in the ring with Carr for twelve rounds, Wharton himself knew what he'd achieved in winning his first professional title.

CHAPTER 6

British Champion

Wharton was starting to earn good purse money now from his career. He reckoned from memory that he cleared £15,000 from the Carr fight (valued at around £27,000 in 2013). He never had any problem receiving his money from Mickey Duff. He'd usually get a cheque within a few days as an interim payment and the remainder arrived a couple of weeks later. Wharton had this to say about those he was involved with: "At the time, when I talk about Mickey Duff and Jarvis Astaire, Terry O'Neill, and the people on board, I loved them all, and I mean that, and a part of me will always love Mickey Duff. He was part of my life, I don't care what others might say about him, I loved the man, he was good to me."

Henry was living with Anita in a house in Leeds, and with daughter Lydia having just arrived the extra money was coming in handy. Extra expense was also being incurred as, perhaps unusually for a boxer, Henry had taken up golf as a way of winding down after training. He'd joined Heworth Golf Club in York and his handicap was coming down quickly. Playing left handed didn't seem to be an issue.

Duff though was determined to make up for lost time and quickly arranged a first defence of the Commonwealth belt four months later on 30 October against Londoner Lou Gent. This was an unexpected choice of opponent. Gent had been, until very recently, a cruiserweight fighting up at a career heaviest of 13st 6lb less than two years previously. He'd twice battled for the British title at that weight, losing inside the distance to both Glen McCrory and Johnny Nelson. In the last twelve months Gent had got down to within a couple of pounds of the super middleweight limit and won three contests, two inside the limit.

Wharton was not only a boxer, but was a boxing fan. He read everything he could on the sport and knew the potential opponents he might have fought in a defence. This is what he learned when he was to fight Gent. "I know he'd been fighting outside his weight division, but he'd found his weight and he was fighting me. I knew it was going to be a tough fight. After what I'd went through with the Carr fight, I was thinking, 'I can't go through that again'."

Wharton was having problems with his damaged knuckle. The first finger of his right hand couldn't fold fully to make a fist, and the slightest touch on the point of the knuckle caused a sharp pain. Every time he punched the heavy bag in the gym, and when he landed solidly while sparring, the pain would increase. Gradually, and without anyone really noticing, his balance in the ring was changing. He would previously have used right handed punches to create a forward momentum, which in turn set up a pivotal motion allowing him to 'load up' with the left hand. Now, because he was reluctant to throw the right, he couldn't get the same power into the left hooks. Terry O'Neill and Gary Atkin were aware that the right hand was painful but not to the extent that they ever believed a bone had been broken. As the fight date approached, each night after training, Henry would attend a physiotherapist in Bradford who used ultra sound in an effort to improve matters, but to no avail. Nevertheless, he was still reasonably confident, and fully committed to keeping the title.

The fight was again in Leeds Town Hall, with Roy Francis refereeing. Immediately prior to the contest Henry decided to approach it differently. Instead of going out intent on finishing it as soon as possible, he chose to be more cautious. Remembering how bad he'd felt during the last fight, aware of the injured right hand and the effect it had on delivering his left hook, he tried to pace himself in anticipation of a long battle.

This turned out to be another momentous struggle for Wharton. Gent's team had done their homework on Henry and the left jab which caused him so many problems before, was the principal weapon in the Londoners' armoury. Time and again it landed cleanly and a lethargic looking champion seemed to be losing his way. With the knowledge of hindsight, it's easy to understand now why the usual Wharton aggression was not in evidence through the first part of the fight. Henry once again relied on his trusted confidante in the corner, Dennie Mancini, to let him know the true progress of the fight. Before the fifth round started Mancini told him he had to 'go'. And 'go' he did! Gent was floored from body shots in each of the next three rounds but he still couldn't stop his tough opponent. Lou recovered well and got back to his controlled boxing, meaning that there were few in attendance who could safely have predicted the outcome. When the bell rang, referee Francis raised Gent's hand and with his supporters thinking their man had won, he walked over quickly to Wharton and did likewise, indicating he'd scored it a draw. There's no doubt that the three knockdowns saved Wharton's crown.

In the immediate aftermath joint managers Duff and O'Neill suggested the fight had came too early following the draining battle with Carr, but they were only partly correct. He had, after all, four months to recover, but the real issue, and to be fair they both were in the dark about it, was the broken bone in the right hand. Was Henry wrong in keeping this to himself? Perhaps the answer lay in the purse for the fight – £34,325 (£62,000 in 2013), almost double the previous fee! Remember, of course, how this would have been broken down in terms of the contract – with expenses taken off the top, followed by 25% being split between Duff and O'Neill as managers, an additional 10% for O'Neill as his trainer, with the remainder going to Henry, and subject to income tax.

In early January 1992, Henry and close buddy, Ron Hopley headed down to London for a spell training at Dennie Mancini's gym in Kings Cross. Also training there at the time were Jim McDonnell who was considering a comeback, super middleweight James Cook and Herol Graham. Wharton had tough sparring at the gym with Bobby Frankham amongst others. Graham had a room next to Ron and Henry in the hotel but unknown to him his two Yorkshire contemporaries didn't like early rises! Around ten o'clock each morning Herol would meet Ron and Henry heading out in their tracksuits and he used to comment on how enthusiastic they were, believing that this was their second run that morning. They didn't have the heart to tell him they weren't as keen as him, and that they had only just got out of bed.

While in London Mickey Duff arranged for Denzil Browne to come down, and he shared a room with them. Putting the three of them together wasn't Duff's best decision! Denzil was only with them for about four days but he must've been a bad influence. They decided to hit the 'town' one night and ended up in Soho. In truth they were looking for a club playing live music where they could sink a couple of pints. All three thought they were pretty wise to the ways of the world and when they passed a doorway with a young 'lady' ushering them into a club charging only £5 admission, they didn't need a second invitation. Our intrepid Yorkshire lads descended into a dingy basement and soon discovered they were the first customers. Very quickly however they were joined by three scantily clad females who handed them drinks menus before sitting down beside them. Denzil was the first to realise they were in the wrong place, and while Henry and Ron were happily ordering coca cola, he noticed the curtains twitching on the small stage and two particularly large gentlemen looking out. He managed to get Henry and Ron's attention and told them it was time to leave. At that, the 'girls' handed over a bill for £90 which drew the expected response from Wharton, who liked to look after his money. It was left to Denzil to negotiate an 'exit' fee with our two Russian bodybuilders, while looking over his shoulder at an increasingly irate Commonwealth champion, and a confused Ron Hopley. Denzil seemed to recall that it cost them £50 to escape.

Henry's next fight had real significance for him because he'd be appearing in his home city of York for the first time as a professional. The Barbican Centre had just opened up and it was considered big enough to cater for the growing army of Wharton supporters. His opponent was Nicky Walker from Carson City, Nevada. He'd fought at the top level but his career was starting to wane. With forty wins from fifty two fights, including two draws, his record was fairly impressive. He'd fought for the IBF super middleweight title in 1988, losing to Graciano Rocchigiani in Germany and a year later lost to former Wharton victim, Frank Minton. He'd lost his last fight to Mike McCallum. This was a financially lucrative fight for all concerned, given that no title was at stake, and Henry's purse was £17,768 (£31,000 / 2013).

In those days Henry's mother's house was virtually a Box Office location for his fights. Mrs Wharton's address and telephone number were publicised in the local press and when fights were announced she would be inundated with people calling for tickets. Many of course went to travellers, and Henry had a cousin in Darlington who regularly brought two busloads of fans from the community up there to his fights.

The Walker fight was an example, albeit unknown to many at the time, of how his right hand was effecting his performance. Although Wharton won convincingly, the fight went the full ten rounds distance and there was no evidence of his much vaunted power. He felt dreadful pain in the right hand every time he threw it, and as a result, he couldn't get the leverage into his left hooks. There was no doubt though that this was forcing him to concentrate more on his boxing skills and he was thinking more about how to create openings. He was aiming punches as opposed to throwing 'bombs' in the general direction of the target.

Mickey Duff could've taken Wharton in a number of directions at the time. The super middleweight division had a series of champions any of whom would have been suitable opponents for Henry, and if he'd been able to bring them to Yorkshire, would've been ensured of filling any venue. Middleweight contests were now completely out of the question for Wharton, making 11st 6lb would've been impossible. In fact making the super middleweight limit was becoming a real challenge.

IBF champion was the fearsome American, Iran Barkley. The WBC champion was Italian, Mauro Galvano, with Victor Cordoba holding the WBA version. The newly recognised WBO had recently witnessed Chris Eubank overcome Michael Watson, in tragic circumstances, and Londoner James Cook was the European champion. Fidel Castro Smith, for good measure, held the British title. We can't forget the ever popular Nigel Benn who was now moving up to super middle after losing his WBO middleweight crown to Chris Eubank. Duff would've had little difficulty in matching Henry with either Cook or Smith, and Galvano could've been a possibility. The others might well have had plans arranged for defences under different promotional banners but there certainly were numerous options available to the wily old manager.

Duff was advised that Henry had to defend his Commonwealth title before anything else, and Henry began looking down the list of fifteen contenders admitting to himself he was concentrating on those at the bottom! He realised he'd be able to fill any hall locally, and that television would buy it, so he secretly hoped for a less than dangerous opponent. It was surprising therefore when Duff suggested a rematch with Rod Carr. Wharton's first reaction was, 'Oh no!', but Duff persuaded him that it was a case of, 'better the devil you know . . . .', so Henry, as always, accepted his manager's advice. The date was set for 8 April at Leeds Town Hall.

Not withstanding the upcoming title fight, Duff was keen on keeping Henry active, and knew that following the Walker fight he could guarantee to fill the Barbican centre in York, and by so doing keep the money flowing in. So only two months after his last fight, on 19 March, Henry was lined up with another American opponent, this time, Kenny Schaefer. Schaefer was a clean cut 'all American boy' from a wealthy Nebraskan family. He'd a good record on paper, winning eighteen of twenty one fights. Two visits to Europe had resulted in stoppage defeats from top performers Tarmo Uusivirta and Christophe Tiozzo. In the build up to the fight Schaefer was training in a gym in York and word was coming back to Henry that he was fast, sharp and really tall. When Henry met him at the weigh in he had concerns about how he could reach up to someone that height. He needn't have worried! In the very first round the back pedalling Schaefer dropped his guard; Wharton hit him with a tremendous left hook and sadly the visitor was unconscious before he hit the ground. The purse was £12,853 (£22,500 in 2013). Kenny Schaefer realised that boxing wasn't for him and retired immediately afterwards.

The second Carr fight was only twenty days after this so in reality the training regime simply continued without a break. Wharton was delighted at this because he knew he'd be fitter and better prepared than he'd ever been. Henry accepted that Carr was physically stronger than him, his right hand was still giving him bother, and making the weight limit was starting to become an issue. Therefore his tactics had to be sound. "I was preparing for a twelve round fight. There was no point in going towards him – he was too strong, he was stronger than me. I couldn't have held him off for twelve rounds. My plan was to box him, take his body away from him and hopefully he tires out."

The fight started off with Carr on the attack, and while Henry had the occasional success he was being beaten to the punch and the left jab was smashing into Wharton's face with alarming regularity. By the halfway stage it was debateable if the champion had won a round. To the neutral observer it appeared Wharton didn't have an answer to the Australians tactics, reinforced by the animated actions of Mickey Duff in the corner who was clearly panicking. However, Terry O'Neill and Dennie Mancini remained calm, and continued encouraging Henry. Wharton can remember saying to his corner men, "Don't worry I'm working on his body." At the end of the sixth, with Duff shouting and screaming, Henry leaned into Mancini and asked, "Am I behind?" The wise old cut man replied, "You've got to go kid, you're behind".

The fight changed in the next round. Wharton's jab began to bang into Carr and several cuts appeared. The crowd sensed the momentum had shifted, and encouraged by this, Henry went for it. Carr was visibly sagging and when the round ended he looked like he'd 'shot his bolt'. In the eighth Wharton shot off his stool and before long the stricken Carr was floored. On rising the referee had seen enough and called the fight off.

An interested spectator sitting at the front of the stage

overlooking the fight was Brendan Ingle and what he'd seen would soon be put to good use.

No sooner had the dust settled than Mickey Duff was again planning the next stage of Wharton's career. The route he chose was the British title held by Fidel Castro Smith, trained by Ingle. Duff had previously suggested Henry could fill an 'open air' venue in Yorkshire, and when the fight was made Henry made it plain he wanted it to be held at the home of his beloved Leeds United. Henry himself can put into his own words how he felt about this. "Being at Elland Road, I'd followed Leeds all my life, I was born just down the road and fighting there for the British championship was just unreal. In my mind I wasn't defending my Commonwealth title but I was fighting for the British title. To come from where I'd come from and to fight for your own national championship is something very, very unique and can't be explained. I just can't explain what it feels like. It's unbelievable."

Terry O'Neill too can remember the local interest and the excitement in the build up to the fight. "There were a lot of Leeds United players who were stars at the time and they got involved. There were photographs with them and they used to come down and watch him spar. The training was again at St Pat's, and in my opinion it was the best gym in England. The main sparring partner was Michael Gale. You couldn't get a better quality kid than Galey. He could turn it on, he could push a fellow back and he had a brilliant left hand. So if you could block his left hand, you could block anybody's." It was obvious from this last comment that Wharton's team knew that Smith's left jab would be an issue. "We also used Nick Manners a bit.

He was tall and he too had a good left hand. Far longer reach than Wharton. I knew Smith was a very good boxer, very accomplished. Really on paper Smith was the favourite. If you looked at the papers they were tipping him to beat Henry."

Gary Atkin, another Leeds man and Leeds United fanatic at the time, can recall the press conference to announce the fight. "Henry and I went out onto the pitch and I remember Gordon Strachan being there and wanting to come to the fight. Lee Chapman – he wanted to come to the fight and they were just building a new massive stand at the ground. It was just incredible. I'd been a Leeds fan since the 1960s and to think we'd be fighting there was unbelievable."

Fidel Castro Smith was a coloured boxer from Nottingham who trained at Brendan Ingle's gym in Sheffield. Ingle could be slightly eccentric and came up with an old Irish name, Slugger O'Toole, for Smith to use when he turned professional. He'd only resorted to his birth name in recent times. He was a very experienced and very skilful boxer. Of his twenty four fights, half of his opponents had failed to hear the final bell. Only three defeats were on his record – and early points loss, a disqualification, and another points defeat in France three and a half years previously. In the intervening period he'd won the British title stopping Ian Strudwick in six rounds and successfully defended it with a points win over former Wharton opponent, Lou Gent.

As the pressure built up, Terry O'Neill took himself and Henry along to Scarborough where they were able to train in private at a local gym there. O'Neill had noticed that Henry was getting distracted back in Leeds and thought the build up was causing him to become too intense, too energetic too soon with the possibility that he might be stale come fight time. Henry used the break in Scarborough to good effect. Although there were training sessions, he found plenty of time just to sit and talk with Terry and very often would wander off on his own. It was at these times he would think through what the fight could mean to him and how important it was for him to do his best on the night and not to let the occasion get to him.

St Pat's gym were preparing for a busy night at Elland Road. Along with Henry they had Tony Silkstone, Nick Manners, Lee Crocker, Phil Epton and Denzil Browne all fighting on the bill. This of course meant that Terry O'Neill and Gary Atkin were preparing four other boxers besides Henry and working with them in the corner. Surprisingly when a boxer is preparing for such a huge fight, Henry had to share the same dressing room as the others, and very often when a boxer left with Terry and Gary the others would go to the arena to watch how they got on, leaving Henry on his own.

In amongst these backstage surroundings emerges another untold tale which helps to explain what life could be like in these circumstances. Nick Manners and Jason Barker, another boxer who wasn't actually fighting that night, were standing in the corridor outside the dressing room, when a well known hard nut and ex heavyweight boxer from Wakefield, Paul Sykes pushed passed security staff into what was supposed to be a private area. Sykes approached Barker and immediately insulted him. Barker and Manners, knowing Sykes' reputation managed to move off without too much difficulty. Shortly after Sykes 'gate crashed' the dressing room area and continued with his derogatory remarks aimed at Manners. Nick, who'd been bandaged up, had heard enough and a left hook knocked the former heavyweight out cold. Not the type of thing the casual spectator would have thought likely just prior to a huge British title fight taking place. The incident didn't seem to effect Manners at all because he stormed out and stopped his opponent Lee Crocker in the very first round, and cheering louder than everyone else at ringside was Sykes.

For his fight Wharton wore a dressing gown and trunks in the colours of Leeds United, made as they always were by O'Neill's wife, Margaret. The fight was on 23 September and with it being well into the autumn there was a slight chill around the large football stadium. Although beginning to struggle to make 12 stones, Henry weighed one and a quarter pounds inside the limit, three-quarters of a pound less than Smith. There were around 8,000 fans in attendance and experienced referee Larry O'Connell was the man in the middle. Harry Carpenter and Frank Bruno were covering the fight for the BBC and Leeds United favourite Eric Cantona was at ringside working with French TV.

During the first half of the fight Wharton showed his boxing skills, jabbing on the way in and picking his shots to Smith's body and head. The British champion was boxing skilfully on the retreat, flicking out left jabs and using his right hand sparingly. Between rounds, Wharton's corner men were using a blanket to keep the night air off their charge. Smith was 'show boating' a little, dropping his hands, posing for ringside photographers, and lifted his right arm above his shoulder on one occasion indicating he was untroubled following a Wharton left hook to the body. The rounds were close and neither man was dominating proceedings but it's likely four of the first six would have gone Wharton's way.

At this stage Terry O'Neill was in no doubt the fight was going to plan and had Wharton ahead. This was reflected in the actions of the corner where even Mickey Duff was relatively calm. O'Neill also took note of the other corner and thought they were becoming a bit anxious. The next four rounds were very similar and close to call. During the tenth Duff was facing the crowd and encouraging them to get behind their man and when that session ended it's probable that referee O'Connell had the fight dead even. Rounds eleven and twelve were huge for Wharton. He came forward throwing punches like a man possessed. Smith looked to be tiring but still tried to fire back and had the occasional success. At the end O'Connell crossed over and raised Wharton's hand to signal that the British title had changed ownership and his Commonwealth crown remained in place. The scorecard read 118-117 meaning the referee had given six rounds to Wharton, four to Smith with two even. As it turned out the final two rounds had clinched it for Henry.

It's always interesting to hear what a fighter's tactics were following an important clash and Wharton revealed what his plan had been. "I was as fit as a fiddle. We planned on throwing more shots to land less, if you can understand what I mean. We made sure we threw five maybe to land two, because of his awkwardness. My punch rate was higher than normal and I made sure I threw more shots. I wasn't bothered about missing, I was more bothered about the ones I was going to land with.

My right hand was still horrendous and I couldn't get full power into the left hand because of it. I was only throwing 'arm' punches with my right."

Wharton felt as the fight entered the latter stages that he was winning and when the bell rang he expected his hand to be raised. Afterwards Smith's trainer Brendan Ingle told Henry that Smith was frustrated with the result because he didn't force the fight enough.

However, there was a massive debate taking place away from ringside among those who'd watched the fight on the BBC and listened to the commentary of Harry Carpenter and Frank Bruno. Both of them, throughout the contest, had Smith well on top and were astounded when the decision came out. Indeed, at one point, Bruno suggested that the only way for Wharton to win on points was if the referee had been bribed! Carpenter apologised for that remark on behalf of Bruno, but nevertheless their commentary created an impression that Smith had been robbed.

Modern day fight fans may not fully appreciate Harry Carpenter's standing in boxing commentary. For decades his was the ONLY voice people could hear when watching boxing on television and naturally enough his opinion came to be respected. It's only when looking back and examining his views on some important fights he commented on that we can consider that perhaps he wasn't the expert people thought he was. Most famously was his reaction at Henry Cooper's last fight against Joe Bugner when the popular Cooper lost a close decision. To listen to Carpenter's outraged views one was encouraged to believe that the result was a travesty. In fact it was a very close fight indeed and the decision could have gone either way.

The Wharton camp had no knowledge of the BBC coverage and were content that they'd thoroughly deserved the win. Wharton can sum up the emotions he felt that night and how Carpenter's and Bruno's comments hit him. "After I won the fight they carried me out the ring with my belt held high and I was a little bit embarrassed and told them to put me down. Such was the emotion of having the British belt. Going back to the dressing room I remember it was absolutely packed. As my bandages were coming off, people were taking them so I signed them. There were fifteen people asking for them but one man got them and he's still got them to this day. We got changed, it was pretty quick, there was a press conference and we went to a pub in Leeds. It was one of the happiest days of my life. The pub was absolutely packed and I was as happy as anything. People came up to me and asked, 'what did you think of that then?'. I asked them what they were meaning and they said, 'that was close wasn't it?'. I said it was always going to be close, Fidel Smith was a good fighter. They then told me that on the telly they had me losing. I thought they were joking. I thought, 'please don't say that.' Then somebody else said the same. I'd watched and read as much boxing as the next man and I know when I've won or lost a fight, and I won that fight. I found myself for the next week explaining myself to people who had watched the telly. No one who'd actually been there had any doubt. It ate into me then and still does and I find myself explaining it to this day. I was so annoyed at the time, and I'd fought so hard to win it I thought about going to the Boxing Board of Control, ask them to get a committee of boxing judges, sit them down and get them to clear this up once and for all. Whatever they decide I'd abide by and if it went against me they could have had my belt. That's how strongly I felt. I'd sooner lose a fight than win by dishonesty. I never asked Mickey Duff for a rematch because I knew I'd won the fight."

There was an unusual twist to the tale a few short weeks later which went some way to calming Henry down. Wharton was invited to Jersey as a guest at an annual amateur match between Yorkshire and Lancashire at the Hotel de France. Unknown to Henry, Harry Carpenter was also a special guest. When Carpenter saw Henry he came over and the first thing he said was, "Will you ever forgive me?" Wharton replied, "You took something I worked all my life for, I dreamed about being British champion, and because of what you said I feel I have to do it all again." He said, "I've watched it back and I was wrong." That meant so much to Wharton and eased the pain he was going through.

Fidel Smith would have two further unsuccessful attempts to win the British title, losing on points both times, and an attempt at the European crown, which similarly ended in failure.

Wharton wouldn't fight for another seven months, but he now held the British and Commonwealth crowns and had put himself right in the mix for world title challenges. He was a well known celebrity in North Yorkshire and featured in the local press regularly. Daughter Lydia had begun toddling about and he was getting a lot of money for doing what he loved, with the potential to earn enough in the next few years to set both himself and his family up for years to come. But, as someone once said jokingly, every silver lining has a cloud, and Henry's cloud was his injured knuckle. He now had to get this attended to, with the inevitable fear that it might be beyond repair.

CHAPTER 7

Leading Contender

When the dust had settled after the Smith fight, Henry knew he couldn't continue with the injured knuckle. He realised his entire training programme and his style of fighting had undergone a gradual and unintentional change by him trying to adapt to throwing a punch with his injured hand. He tried to minimise the pain when landing by trying to make sure it was the outside edge of the glove making contact. Because he couldn't put the full force into punching with the right hand, the countering swing from the left side of his body, which he needed to generate full power, simply couldn't be achieved. It was with a great degree of reluctance he eventually confided to Terry O'Neill and Mickey Duff that the hand was broken, and the services of Mr Rushman would again need to be engaged.

The surgeon operated, and yet another pin was inserted in the right hand, with the right index finger fixed temporarily at a ninety degree angle. Meantime the WBC, as a result of his win over Smith, installed Wharton as the number one contender for Nigel Benn's crown. When this was announced Mickey Duff had several discussion with both Henry and Terry O'Neill about what this meant in terms of his British title. Duff told them that the Boxing Board would order Henry to defend it, and that could have two outcomes. Firstly it might delay the fight with Benn as Wharton would be required to fight whoever the Board nominated, and secondly, if he took on a challenge to Benn, and couldn't accommodate the boxer the Board proposed, then that person would have to be paid money to 'step aside'.

On 7 April at Leeds Town Hall another Nebraskan, Ray Domenge, was the unsuspecting victim of a rejuvenated Henry Wharton. Once in the gym and injury free, Henry was back to his best, punching at full power with both hands. Fellow Americans Troy Watson and Tim Johnson had pulled out beforehand and they would never have known how lucky they were. Domenge had a respectable record winning eleven of fifteen fights and had never been halted. He would later demonstrate his durability by taking the legendary Roberto Duran to a points decision as well as stopping previous Wharton victim, Frank Minton. Domenge weighed 11st 11lb, almost half a stone lighter than Wharton who was delighted at not having to make the super middleweight limit. Domenge lasted until the third round, when on going down for a second time from left hooks, was stopped by Mickey Vann.

In March and June, Benn made successful voluntary defences of his world title, and knowing that a mandatory challenge from Wharton was being delayed, Duff tried to keep Henry busy by arranging another fight on 19 May in Sunderland against Royan Hammond, but the York man fell down with flu and had to call-off the fight.

Henry, although he was desperate to fight for the world crown, because that was his ultimate ambition, nevertheless, was so proud at being the British champion, and wanted the Lonsdale Belt to keep. He would have taken the 'British' route if the decision had been left solely to him. But with a fight with

Benn looking increasingly likely Mickey Duff advised the Board
that Henry was giving up his British belt. The first Wharton
knew that he'd relinquished the British title was when he heard
that James Cook and Fidel Smith were to contest the vacant
crown. He had never given the final word to Duff that he was
willing to give it up, it just seemed to happen.

The match with Hammond eventually did go ahead on 1 July
and Henry was delighted to appear again in front of his home
fans at the Barbican Centre. Duff had managed to find another
American with a reasonable record but who should not have
caused Wharton many problems. He'd seventeen wins from
twenty three fights but most had been in the light middle or
middleweight divisions. Britain's Richie Woodhall had beaten
Hammond on points in April.

Again Mrs Wharton had been selling tickets from the house
and they went like 'hot cakes'. The Barbican Centre was full to
capacity and surprisingly Wharton weighed in three pounds
lighter than Hammond who was a career heaviest at 12st 4lb. It
was a sluggish start from Wharton but he got some inspiration
between the second and third rounds. One of his corner men
heard Hammond's trainer telling their fighter that Wharton was
a 'pussycat'. The comment acted on Henry like a 'light bulb
getting switched on'. Part way through the round Wharton
backed towards the ropes deliberately trying to bring
Hammond forward. Once he came within range the York man
unleashed a five punch combination and the fight was over.
Wharton's purse for this fairly routine outing was £10,000
(£17,000 in 2013).

As far as Wharton was concerned this would be his last bout

before a world title challenge to Nigel Benn, and that was an entirely logical perspective. He'd been Benn's mandatory challenger for over nine months. In that time, since winning the championship in October 1992, Benn had made three successful defences including a contracted return fight with the man he won it from, Mauro Galvano. Nevertheless, in boxing, money is king. The ever popular puncher, Benn, was anxious to avenge a previous defeat by Chris Eubank for the WBO middleweight crown in 1990, and the entire British boxing fraternity wanted to see him try.

Eubank had been managed and promoted brilliantly, fighting regularly on the new SKY satellite channel often against less than worthy opposition, but for huge sums. The boxing public disliked his posturing and arrogance but had to acknowledge his strength, speed and ring tactics. He'd remained unbeaten since the start of his career and there were many who would have paid good money to see him get his 'come-uppence' especially from Nigel Benn.

Sadly for Henry a Eubank/Benn fight for the combined WBO and WBC titles just had to happen. Both boxers and their teams would earn huge purses, the television company who covered the fight would surpass previous viewing figures for live boxing, and the sanctioning bodies could fill their coffers. The fact that Henry was the number one contender seemed to matter not one jot.

When that fight was announced Henry wasn't surprised. He suspected the public clamour would sway the decision makers. Duff however was incensed and immediately contacted the WBC to protest. It fell on deaf ears and the world title fight was set for Old Trafford on 9 October.

Duff knew that he'd a good case to get something out of the mess by claiming 'step aside' money from the WBC. This had been a fairly recent development within boxing, when the organisations seemed to have breached their own rules, and sought to compensate an aggrieved party. At the same time Duff realised that regardless of what transpired at Old Trafford, Henry wouldn't get his title shot for some months thereafter, so he arranged another fight in the meantime, two days before the Benn v Eubank battle, and again at the popular Barbican Centre.

Once again Duff had to be careful when selecting a suitable opponent. One who would satisfy both the Board of Control and the boxing public, but would not put Henry's number one ranking in jeopardy. On this occasion, up stepped yet another American foe in the shape of Ron Amundsen. Although Amundsen was on the slide, he'd stepped up from light middle and had fought the best. He lost inside the distance to Roy Jones but took both James Toney and Vinny Pazienza the full course. He'd also lost on points in Italy to Gianfranco Rosi for the IBF world title and more recently visited the UK losing over ten rounds to Nicky Piper. He seemed to meet Duff's criteria.

This turned out to be an excellent contest, with Amundsen determined to give his all. Wharton looked relaxed and confident but the fighting Mormon from Chicago ensured that the local man didn't let his attention wander. On occasion Henry would move back onto the ropes and allow Amundsen to throw punches with both hands, giving him a chance to demonstrate sharp defensive skills. Wharton paced himself, letting heavy punches go in short bursts then stepping back and blocking counters, thereby conserving energy. Several times, particularly in the sixth, Amundsen looked to be on the way out but he fought back bravely. Finally, midway through the eighth round, a solid right landed causing the American to stagger slightly and when Wharton moved forward the referee, perhaps a shade prematurely, stepped in to end the by now, one sided contest. Henry earned £10,000, but more importantly he banked another eight valuable rounds against a very experienced boxer who'd resisted his big punches in the early part of the fight and made him work for his purse.

Two nights later Terry O'Neill and Gary Atkin joined Henry and 42,000 others at Old Trafford for the Nigel Benn/Chris Eubank fight. Contrary to what most people might have expected, Henry remembers clearly going to the fight simply as a boxing fan. It seemed the entire boxing world was there and he was just as excited as the next man. As the fight was progressing he recalls discussing how it was going with those around him and they all reckoned it was close. As the fight was moving into the last third Henry suddenly realised that he'd most likely be fighting the winner, and had a good laugh at himself getting caught up in the atmosphere without being consciously aware of the implications in the future for himself. He hadn't been paying attention to how both boxers were performing and was jumping up and down with those around him. It's an endearing characteristic of Wharton that he simply didn't comprehend that he himself was a celebrity, he just thought of himself as another boxing fan out for a good night's entertainment.

After an enthralling battle, which swung one way then the other, the fight was scored a draw, with two judges giving it alternatively to Benn and Eubank by seven rounds to five and the third making it six rounds each. This result meant that Eubank kept his WBO title and the WBC belt remained with Benn.

The tragic splintering of world titles was no more pronounced than at this stage in the super middleweight division. As we've seen, Eubank and Benn held their versions, but across the Atlantic, James Toney was the IBF champion while Michael Nunn wore the WBA belt. Potentially, Mickey Duff could have taken either route and Henry would have been an acceptable proposition for any of the governing bodies. But he was committed to challenging for the WBC title, and to be fair, that organisation was probably the most prominent. The Benn fight would be the easiest to make and most lucrative for all involved.

At long last Henry was being given a chance to fulfil a lifetimes ambition, and that of his dad Billy, who had predicted as a youngster he'd be a world champion one day. It was a long, long way from picking fruit in Wisbech and sharing a caravan with twelve others for nine months every year.

CHAPTER 8

Build-up to the Benn Fight

By November Don King and Frank Warren had won the purse bids for the Benn and Wharton world title fight. When the announcement was made at the Marriott Hotel, Marble Arch in London Henry knew he'd made 'the big time'. Reports came out that Wharton's share of the purse would be £365,000 (£615,000 in 2013). There's a story surrounding the purse bids demonstrating how cunning Duff could be. The bids had to be put inside sealed envelopes and only opened when the deadline passed. Duff had let it be known in the relevant circles that he was desperate to promote the fight because Wharton was such a huge 'ticket seller'. When Duff's envelope was opened it was apparently for the paltry sum of £80,000. The winning bid was reported to have been £1,000,000!

This was the type of fight Duff had been planning since his relationship with Wharton first began in the Grosvenor Casino all those years ago. It was also hugely satisfying for Terry O'Neill who'd dedicated his life to training boxers, many of whom had won amateur titles and made international appearances, but none had reached this pinnacle. Duff had regularly been involved at this level and new what was required in terms of preparation, but for Henry and Terry it was something special and unique.

This was also a huge step up financially for Wharton and

O'Neill. Terry would be due half of the 25% managers cut as well as 10% trainers fee, but for both, it meant more than that. It was about recognition, and acceptance amongst their peers that they were 'world class'. Nobody should diminish Gary Atkin's role in this either. He had been with Henry in the gym since he first arrived at St Patrick's. He'd pounded the streets with him, held the pads in the ring, been in the dressing room before the fights and had become a close and trusted friend. It's important to boxers to have people they can trust and rely on by their side.

Mickey Duff suggested that a camp should be set up in America, and as far as Henry was concerned this idea was like pushing against an open door. He always wanted to see a bit of the world, different places, and was delighted with the suggestion. O'Neill had reservations, not least of which was due to the fact his wife Margaret was battling cancer. Gary Atkin too would have preferred that Henry got his fitness to a certain level at home in Leeds prior to travelling out for specialised sparring shortly before the fight. Also, Henry's partner Anita was heavily pregnant with their second child, and of course, Christmas was fast approaching.

In the end, all agreed that the benefits outweighed the disadvantages and the decision was taken to go out to the States. Gary Atkin had taken his honeymoon in Florida that August, and spent it at a friend, Vince Campbell's, house at Davenport in Polk County. He felt it was ideally situated as a base for all three to stay and, in addition, he knew there were suitable routes near at hand for them to go running. Of course the most important factor was the weather. They all knew that it was guaranteed to be at least mild, far better than what could be expected back home. Terry O'Neill had an unenviable and agonising decision to make. On the one hand there was an opportunity to run a training camp in the build up to a world title fight, but against this was the thought of leaving his wife while she was fighting serious illness. In the end up it was his devoted wife Margaret who made the decision for him – "you're going, I'll be fine".

Wharton flew out with Mickey Duff to Las Vegas to argue the case for compensation with the WBC because Nigel Benn had fought Eubank instead of him. Henry remembered the procedure was similar to a court hearing. "We're in the room and he's (Benn) put his case forward. I asked 'where do I stand?' He's had a million and half for his defence when he should have been defending against me, and I said 'what's going on?'. They set a price and I said that was no good to me. I asked for my percentage of his million and a half pounds. Anyway, Nigel Benn came over to me and he said, 'Let me tell you something as a friend. Take the money.' I told him it was all right for him to say that as he had his money from the Eubank fight. He said, 'Do yourself a favour and take the money, they won't give you any more.' In the end I took what was offered, we shook hands, had a cuddle, and off we went our separate ways." The sum reported at the time was US$ 50,000.(about £42,000 at 2013 values).

While Henry and Duff were in Las Vegas, on 18 December O'Neill and Atkin flew to Orlando and checked in at Vince Campbell's house. They'd been given some boxing gyms to visit nearby, and eventually settled for the Police Athletic League gym in Winter Haven ran by an old 'boxing' man Jack Leonard.

When Henry met up with them, they quickly got down to business. Terry, through liaising with Mickey Duff in London, organised sparring partners to support local Floridian, Troy Watson, who was a top quality fighter in his own right. Watson arrived on the twenty seventh, with Jo Jo Harris arriving a day later. By that time Henry had already cut Watson's eye in sparring an injury which had to be stitched at a local hospital.

The gym was very good, it had everything a training camp could need. The early mornings runs were ideal, even though, surprisingly for Florida, Gary can remember frost being on the ground. However, Winter Haven, the area where the gym was situated, was not your typical 'Disney destination!'. Henry and Gary got the local perspective when they visited a hairdresser nearby. The girl who was cutting their hair remarked that it was unusual to have English people there at that time of year. Gary told them what they were about and explained where they were training. The girl was shocked and remarked that if she was driving her car near there, and the traffic lights turned to red, she wouldn't stop! As it turned out the girl knew what she was talking about.

On 6 January videos of Benn's fights arrived with the team giving them something to do in the evenings. Henry also managed to squeeze in the odd game of golf at the nearby Oaklands club.

What happened next, after only a couple of weeks in Florida is, unsurprisingly, etched in Gary Atkin's memory for all time. He tells the story well. "We had a big black lad come in the gym, and there were two coaches there who had the gym and they

were both sat in rocking chairs. A black man and a white man.
One of them was Jack Leonard. Henry was shadow boxing this
day and the big black kid is asking me what we were doing. I
told him we were training to fight Nigel Benn for the world title.
I thought he might have been a boxer, he was a big athletic lad.
So we did the sparring and the sparring partner disappeared. So
I'm sat there with my vest on and shorts looking at the watch.
Henry is on the three step thing beside the ring with dumb bells
in his hands going up and down. We were just finishing off. The
doors get booted in. There was two of them, six foot plus, with
their guns out. I froze. I just sat there. Henry kept on stepping
up, sweat pumping out of him. On the floor they said. One put
a gun to Terry's head and the other put his gun to my head. It
went through my head, 'I've just got married, she's pregnant,
and I'm never going to see them again. I was actually thinking
what it would feel like when the bullet hits my head. I've got my
wallet but because I've got shorts on they don't think I've got
anything. But they took Terry's wallet off him. It had his
mothers wedding ring I think and some small personal photos
and the address we were staying at. When they left the two fellas
in the rocking chairs never moved as if it happened every day.
Henry and I just looked at each other as if we couldn't believe
what happened. It was quiet and then the doors burst open
again. They'd come back because they hadn't got enough and
they were demanding more money. I thought they'd come back
to kill us because we'd seen them. Anyway they left and the
police were called. This great big black policeman arrived and
he had a Mack on like 'Columbo'. I couldn't believe it. The
detective asked what type of guns they had, and I told them they

had a revolver and an automatic. He said 'how do you know, you don't have guns in England'. I told him I had seen guns on the telly. He then began pulling out guns from everywhere and saying, 'was it one of these?', then, 'was it one of these?'. He even had one down his sock, I couldn't believe it. We didn't even get showered, we're in the car and we're off. Back at the digs. We had something to eat and Henry always liked to go a walk after eating. He said 'I'm not happy here' and I totally agreed with him. I phoned Mickey up and told him Henry wasn't happy here. He tried to get us to stay on. The next thing the phone rang and its the BBC. I think Mickey got about £3,000 for telling the story to the media. That night before bed time I goes into Henry's room and says 'see you in the morning'. I looked at the bottom of the bed, and I said, 'you've got shoes on.' I lifted the bed covers and he was fully dressed. 'Gaz' he says, 'they took the wallet and the address is in it, if I hear that door going I'm straight out that window.' So I realised then we had to get out of Florida."

All involved can see the funny side to the story now because it was so unreal. It's simply unbelievable that a boxer, and his entourage, training for a world title fight, a huge event at least in the UK, could be held up at gunpoint in their gym in the middle of the day. If Don King had set it up as a publicity stunt he'd have been laughed out of town! At the time though, it was far from comical. Gary Atkin had already questioned the wisdom of starting a training camp so long before the fight. Terry O'Neill had his wife back home battling cancer and Henry's second child was due anytime. Now they'd been robbed at gunpoint!

Mickey Duff was persuaded that the American sojourn was at an end, and he quickly showed his ability to act swiftly. Duff used his worldwide network of contacts and within a day or two he'd secured the use of the Hotel Paraiso in Estepona, Spain. They flew from Orlando to Miami, then to Madrid and onwards to Malaga with principal sparring partner, Troy Watson, alongside.

Once in Spain, as should be expected, it took some time to get all the arrangements in place. The main issue was that there wasn't a boxing ring. In terms of sparring, although Troy Watson came with them, other sparring partners had to be flown out including Paul Wright, Marvin O'Brien and Ali Forbes. Initially the group managed to use a boxing ring under the stand at the local Marbella Football Club before they hired a ring from a local boxing gym. This proved to be totally unsuitable so Duff had to have one driven out from England. Thereafter the training settled down into a routine and progressed very well indeed. The training facilities at the hotel couldn't have been better. They were allocated an area inside an open air conservatory and were often watched by fascinated hotel guests.

On 9 February, as part of the build up, twenty five reporters and camera men turned up from Britain and this brought it home to everyone just how big the fight was, and that it was approaching rapidly.

As fight time approached the tension was building daily. Henry had been training for almost ten weeks without a break. He'd been watching his food intake but was still having difficulty getting his weight down. His son was due any day, and he hadn't seen Anita or his family since they left the UK.

Eventually the 'pot boiled over'. One night after dinner Henry disappeared. Gary walked down into Estepona looking for his charge, and found him in a local bar having a pint. Atkin's first reaction was to get him back to the hotel because he knew that his weight was an issue. However, he quickly realised that Henry was near breaking point. Both of them settled down for the night and had a 'skin full'. As Atkins admits, 'it wasn't very professional, but it got him relaxed and he got his head back on'.

On 15 February the camp returned home and Henry moved into Oulton Hall Hotel on the outskirts of Leeds. Anita moved into the hotel with them and the very first night, with heavy snow falling outside, she went into labour, and because she'd been attending the maternity hospital in York, Henry got up and drove through the wintry conditions to get there. Later that morning Henry junior was born. Meanwhile, back at Oulton Hall Gary Atkin was in a blind panic because when he went to Henry's room to get him for training he'd disappeared. However the birth of Henry junior took a lot of pressure off him, and when he returned to the hotel he felt a lot better.

The big fight build up had begun in earnest. The promoters were reporting that all 11,700 tickets for Earls Court had sold out. The fight was being shown live on ITV and it was being predicted that viewing figures would top the 16.5 million who had tuned in for the Benn – Eubank fight. The bookmakers were starting to lay odds. William Hill's had Benn the 4-11 favourite with Henry the outsider at 2-1. It was estimated that Henry's fans had bought in excess of 3,000 tickets. The local Yorkshire press were covering the build up on a daily basis with special editions of their newspapers being produced. Wharton seemed

totally unfazed with all the attention. He willingly gave interviews to all who asked, and even had time to show off his new
$150 hinged gum shield he had been made for him by a dentist
in Orlando.

The odds favouring Benn were not surprising. He was a
boxing superstar. An ex-soldier he'd been an ABA champion and
exploded onto the professional scene destroying a whole host of
opponents with his thrilling 'all or nothing' fighting style. In his
first two years he stormed through twenty two fights winning
them all inside the distance and captured and defended the
Commonwealth middleweight title in the process. When Benn
fought, the question being asked was not if he would win, but
if his opponent would last the distance. Benn's smashing,
bashing victory run was halted in May 1989 when the superb
Michael Watson absorbed all the early punishment, firing back
to halt Benn in the sixth round, to annex his crown.

Benn's backers then decided to take him to America and in
his next five fights he faced sterner opposition who managed, in
the main, to take his heavy punches and provided him with the
opportunity to pace himself more. The last fight in the States
was a one round demolition of the fearsome Iran Barkley. This
allowed him to fight for a world title for the first time in a grudge
match with Chris Eubank. Again, he fought a skilful, and
strong, defensive boxer who stopped him in the ninth round.

Benn was struggling now to make the middleweight limit
and his move up to 12st proved successful when he went to Italy
on 3 October 1992 and won the WBC title, by stopping Mauro
Galvano. Since then, he'd defended against Nicky Piper, made
a successful return defence against Galvano, beaten former

Wharton foe, Lou Gent, stopping the fellow Londoner in the fourth. Then he had the recent drawn fight with Eubank for the unified championship.

In all Benn had won thirty seven of forty fights, thirty three inside the distance, and quite possibly was at the peak of his career. He was now being trained by Jimmy Tibbs and was undoubtedly a more skilful boxer who'd come to realise that he couldn't knock everyone out in the first few rounds. That's not to suggest however that he'd lost any of his knockout punching power, it's just that the more capable opponents didn't invite a punch on the chin!

Like Wharton, Benn had gone abroad to prepare, in his case to his own training camp in Playa de Las Americas, Tenerife. Rumours had began circulating that he was considering retirement in the near future and there was unfounded speculation that perhaps he was not treating Wharton as a dangerous opponent. It's probably the case that this was 'paper talk' simply to fuel discussion amongst the boxing fraternity. In Benn's autobiography he described in detail his training regime which consisted of daily training runs at high altitude on Mount Teide followed by gym work with his trainer, Jimmy Tibbs. Nowadays top boxers have nutritionists on board but in the mid 1990s this was relatively unusual. Benn had travelled to America to consult such a person and in his training camp in Tenerife he was taking one hundred and twenty vitamin and supplement pills a day. It didn't seem that Benn was taking Wharton lightly at all.

Extravagant principal promoter Don King arrived from America to beat the drum and stir up added interest in the big fight. He got permission from the British Boxing Board to stage the weigh in at the offices of the Law Society in Chancery Lane and arranged a final press conference at the House of Commons.

Of course the Wharton family travelled to London for the fight. Henry's mother and sisters had been booked into the same hotel, the Kensington Palace, as the team, but when they arrived they discovered that Mickey Duff had taken their room. He'd made alternative arrangements for them however, but when they visited the next hotel the reception desk had no idea who they were. When they got back to the Kensington Palace, Henry had to have a word with the reception to get them in. But Mrs Wharton's troubles didn't end there. She had a routine she used to do for all of Henry's fights. She would pack his bag, putting the boots in first, followed by a brand new, and freshly washed towel. Thereafter, to give him energy, she would also put in iced buns. She knows the whole thing sounds ridiculous now, but it was just a sort of lucky custom which she didn't want to break. She went out and bought a new, white towel and arranged for the hotel staff to wash it. They lost it, and eventually Mrs Wharton had to make do with a hotel towel. But the buns were OK!

It's interesting to learn what the genuine views of the Wharton camp were in the few days before the first punch was thrown. Terry O'Neill was supremely confident. "I was 99% certain that Henry would beat him. I thought Henry would be too strong and that Benn was on the way down. I honestly thought Henry would stop him." Gary Atkin was similarly minded. "Henry was looking good. He was punching like a heavyweight. I had no doubt he'd win. Both were big punchers and I couldn't see the fight going the distance. So I thought Henry would stop him." Henry can also remember his own thoughts. "I was a great fan of Nigel Benn, I'd followed his career. I knew he was the champ, but I honestly thought I'd beat him. I thought I'd stop him. The seventh round was always when I seemed to get my second wind. I thought I might win the fight around that stage. I'm not a boastful person, it's not in my nature. But I was confident in my own ability, I thought I'd win."

Wharton however suffered from the boxers curse. He'd trouble making the weight. On the night before the weigh in, 24 February, the group went to the Peacock gym in Canning Town with the intention of having a light training session. When they got there they discovered that Henry was five and half pounds over the limit. On went the sweat suit and the next few hours were spent skipping and shadow boxing. It was not enough. The next day the team travelled to Chancery Lane and arrived an hour before the officials. Henry jumped on the scales with only Gary and Terry for company and to their horror he was still two and half pounds over. Henry then found some bin bags and put them on under his training gear and proceeded to run round the lanes surrounding the Law Society. He eventually came in half a pound under the limit.

Duff had booked seats in a very up market restaurant called Sale-e-Pepe in Knightsbridge straight after the weigh in and completely by coincidence Frank Warren and Don King came in and sat at a table next to them. Thereafter Duff took Henry, Terry and Gary to Earls Court to scan the venue and were able to watch Mike Goodall and his staff putting up the ring. The scene was now set for the biggest night in Henry's boxing career.

CHAPTER 9

The Benn Fight

It might be considered unusual to start the report on a world title fight by going straight to the judges scorecards following the completion of the twelve rounds. Nevertheless, by starting at the end and working back we may be better placed to form a clearer picture in our minds of how the fight progressed.

At the outset, it is only right and proper to point out that those in the busy ring waiting for the official announcement, including Wharton and his corner men, already knew Benn had retained his crown. That was not in doubt.

Welsh judge Adrian Morgan scored the bout 116 – 113, English judge Sid Nathan had it 116 – 114, and Californian judge Rudy Ortega, made it 117 – 112, all in favour of the winner. But let's look at the implications of the scoring in more detail.

At the end of the fifth round, Wharton had caught Benn with a stunning shot and the follow up punches put the champion over. The referee took up the count and Benn didn't seem to be in any difficulty. The bell sounded before the fight could recommence. Normally when a knockdown occurs the boxer who hits the canvas usually loses the round 10 – 8. On this occasion, because there was some dispute about whether Benn had actually been knocked over or had simply stumbled, and due to the fact that it was so near the end of the round, it is likely the judges only gave the round to Wharton 10 – 9. If this was indeed the case, then Morgan had Benn winning the fight seven rounds to four with one round scored a draw. Nathan gave eight rounds to Benn and four to Wharton and Ortega had it eight rounds to Benn, three to Wharton and one even.

What is the significance of all this?

Well, it's pretty certain that Benn easily won the first four rounds. He moved and jabbed repeatedly, occasionally letting the right hand go, and was in total control. Henry, meanwhile, shuffled round the ring eating left jabs and hardly landed a clean shot. That being the case, this then signifies that during the last two thirds of the fight, eight rounds, Morgan gave four to Wharton, three to Benn with one scored a draw. Sid Nathan would have given Benn and Wharton four rounds each and Rudy Ortega would have scored them four rounds to Benn, three to Wharton, with one even. Therefore over the last eight rounds the fight was a draw.

During those final few rounds Benn was tiring, while Henry was still ploughing forward in search of a knockout. Wharton had a fair amount of fuel left in the tank, but Benn was emptying quickly. Benn and his team are to be congratulated though, because at the end of a world title fight the gauge should be pointing to empty, that is how it should be. There's no point in saving your energy, you've got to use it all to win the fight. If Henry had something in reserve then perhaps he should have gone for it far sooner than he did. It was a twelve round fight not an eight rounder, the result is in the history books and there are no complaints from Henry, Terry O'Neill or Gary Atkin. Henry lost fair and square.

Let's now look at the fight from the beginning.

Terry O'Neill has a clear recollection of the circumstances on the night of the fight. "Mickey Duff said we've got to go to the venue and we were there four hours before the fight. We were in this hut thing near the venue and all you could hear was this constant drone, 'Henry, Henry', 'Benn, Benn', that went on and on and on. But then the walk from there to the ring was unbelievable. There were all sorts going on. There were cans getting thrown and folk shouting 'Wharton go home' and 'Benn's going to knock you out' all that sort of thing and the intimidation was there. Remember this was the first big event really for Henry and going into a world title fight with someone like Benn with his reputation and with all this happening around him, his mind was just not focussed on the job. In my mind there all sorts going on in the background which shouldn't have been happening because for three or four rounds he just wasn't with it."

Gary Atkin had similar memories of the accommodation at Earls Court. "The dressing rooms were basic, they were port-a-cabins. There seemed to be no control over who was allowed in there. Kirkland Laing came in and he was blind drunk, showing everybody how to throw a jab and all that sort of thing. We asked Mickey to try to get him out. On the way to Earls Court it was like a rugby international, there were fans with flags everywhere. Henry and I when we were in the taxi going there and seeing all fans we actually wished it was us going to watch the fight!"

During the early part of the fight Benn looked relaxed and composed. Gone were the days when he exhausted himself trying to knock opponents out with every punch he threw. He was much more controlled. He moved from side to side and feinted trying to create openings. This forced Wharton to cover up and when he did Benn threw the big punches generally to the torso.

Henry hardly landed a worthwhile punch throughout the first twelve minutes of the contest. In the third he opened up and although his fans got excited not one of the swinging hooks caught Benn cleanly.

Wharton can recall his thoughts going into the ring and how he felt as the fight progressed. "There's nothing wrong with taking punches, all your life you do. But you never know if you can take that ferocity from someone like Benn. You simply don't know that. It's all very well after the fight saying he couldn't put me down. Now I know he couldn't put me down but I didn't know beforehand. There weren't many in the world who could take his punches. I was never ever frightened of anybody, but I was cautious. Mickey Duff always said 'if your in the fight, you can win it', and that's the way I was playing it, caution, caution. Another thing Mickey used to say was, 'There's a danger when you start too slow that you can't get going.' That was the danger for me and it happened. I was trying to rev myself up in the corner, the were screaming at me."

As far as the paying public were concerned, at least those who were supporting Wharton, the fight only started at the fifth round. Just before the bell sounded Dennie Mancini was bawling into Henry's ear in an obvious attempt to rouse him, but it was a vicious right uppercut from Benn followed by a punch after the referee ordered them to stop which finally got him into gear. At long last he went on to the front foot. It looked like he'd thrown a weight off his shoulders and he got down to business. The crowd could sense it and just before the bell a short left hook from Wharton landed on Benn's chin. Until people could see the slow-motion replay of the punch landing it would probably only have been Wharton and Benn who realised that the champion was momentarily stunned. Benn staggered briefly and a cuffing left hook from Henry, landing on the top of his head, caused him to touch down. The referee gave him a standing count but it was obvious that he'd recovered his senses.

The next round was a thriller. Benn, perhaps unsettled by the count, resorted to the 'Benn of old', ditching the skilful boxing plan and tore into Wharton. The Yorkshire man, full of self belief, throwing caution to the wind put everything into his punches. The crowd were on their feet and at last they had a world title fight worthy of the name. The seventh was very similar and any tactics either boxer had before the fight went out the window.

The doubts Wharton had about being able to withstand the Benn punch were well and truly put to the test early in the eighth. Coming off the ropes the champion threw his 'Sunday punch' and it landed cleanly on the left side of Wharton's face, knocking his lovely new gum shield across the ring for the second time during the fight. Henry's legs dipped and in the split second it took his senses to return another shot was partially blocked. When the referee called a halt to have the gum shield put back in Wharton could be seen winking at his corner to let them know he was fine. Benn dominated the remainder of the round but both boxers now knew they had landed their

best punches, and had caused their opponents real problems. At
the same time they also knew they could survive a full blooded
blow without the fear of being knocked out. This meant that
Benn and Wharton could take chances over the last four rounds.

The ninth and tenth were good rounds for Wharton. He
tried to open Benn up with jabs and now moving forward was
getting his shots off. Benn was doing a lot of bobbing and
weaving along the ropes with the occasional right cross being
thrown as he sprang off them. The feeling from the ITV
commentary team of Jim Watt and Reg Gutteridge was that the
rounds were now very close but of great importance was the fact
that Benn had clearly won the first four.

The final two rounds had the entire Earls Court crowd on
their feet as the fight swung one way then another. Both these
rounds were very hard to score as the boxers put all their effort
into every punch. When the final bell rang all those in
attendance had to acknowledge that they'd seen a really good
contest. Commentators Gutteridge and Watt felt Benn had won
and from ringside Barry McGuigan, on his unofficial scorecard,
had Benn winning 115 – 114. When interviewed on the ring
apron immediately after the fight Benn said that Wharton had
been his strongest opponent and added that he'd benefited from
tough fights with Eubank, Watson and de Witt. Henry
meanwhile noted that world champions like Benn were able to
change tactics during a fight and that he would gain from this
experience.

Looking back at the fight all these years later this is what
Wharton feels about the contest now, and also what he can
remember thinking when it was actually taking place. "I was in

the fight, and in a lot of the fights before Benn I came late. I had worked hard and I was prepared. I was never in doubt about myself and I thought I'd find a way, and in the fifth round, when I knocked him down I got up off the stool with a little bit more intent. I said, 'come on' lets pick it up now.' Even though the corner had been screaming at me I just couldn't get going. I don't know what it was that night. I could see punches coming and he wasn't hurting me but I just couldn't get going. Maybe I gave him too much respect early on and I couldn't shake it off. In the sixth round when I came out I was a changed man. But there are those who've said Benn had a glass chin, but let me tell you he hasn't got a glass jaw. I hit him with some really good shots that would have knocked mere mortals out. In the past I'd knocked others out with those shots but I didn't knock Benn out. At the end I could have gone on another four rounds easily, but because I'd given Benn a lead I just couldn't catch up. Benn's style didn't suit me. It would have suited me if he came at me the way he did years ago, when he was the first Nigel Benn. Because he'd learned, he was clever and he used that. I remember going into the last two rounds believing that I could still knock him out. One clean shot and I could've knocked him out. When the final bell rang I felt I'd won the last two rounds and was right there, in it. It was now down to how the judges saw it. Sometimes the result filters into the ring before the official announcement but nobody told me anything. But Benn did a kind of mini celebration and from that moment I didn't think positive again. I think someone had given him the nod. All these years later I can hardly speak about how I felt when they announced the result, the floor opened up. I was worse than gutted. I was numb, if someone had stuck something in me I wouldn't have felt it. I remember going and sitting somewhere myself and I couldn't believe what had happened to me. I'll tell you, when I was in the hotel room before the fight, because the world championship meant so much to me, I had nightmares that I wouldn't be ready. Even today I still have dreams about fighting someone for the world title and in my dreams I'm telling myself, 'he can't beat me, I'm going to be world champion, but I won't be ready in time', and I wake up sweating. Something left me that night and part of my life changed. Even at the press conference afterwards, and I swear this is the truth, I'm looking along the table and Benn was there, he had his belt, Steve Little (who also won a version of the world title that night) had his belt, and I'm thinking there's something wrong here, they're mine. I know it's daft but I'm thinking those belts are mine. I hated sitting there. I'd earned a lot of money, but it absolutely meant nothing to me, nothing!"

That memory, but more importantly, his feelings which still exist today some twenty years after the fight, demonstrate what boxing meant to Wharton. It was all about winning. Yes, he liked the money because that allowed him to be independent and it opened doors to luxuries he never dreamt of when he was growing up in a caravan picking fruit in Wisbech. But personal pride, and sense of achievement, meant so much more. He could recall his father telling him in his teens that he'd be a world champion. Bill Brown and Terry O'Neill recognised from a very early age he had a special talent. He was born with a knockout punch and that had taken him into amateur internationals, the British and Commonwealth titles as a professional, but the pinnacle, and proof of his talent, would have been the world championship.

For ten weeks or so he'd been in a training camp away from his family and friends and had never been better prepared for a fight. To then fail at the final hurdle must have been like losing someone close to you. The initial pain might lessen through time, but the void would always be with you, and that's what happened to Henry. It must have felt like a climber about to swing his ice axe onto the summit of Everest just when a gust of wind blows him a hundred feet back down the mountain.

Benn's trainer, Jimmy Tibbs, told the press, "Nigel was superb, absolutely brilliant. Even better then when he fought Chris Eubank. That's the best he's ever fought since I've been with him. At times I had to pinch myself to remember I wasn't watching Sugar Ray Leonard." Benn, embarrassed with the praise added, "He's a strong boy, he wanted to fight. But I underestimated him. I didn't think he could punch that hard. I think he'll learn from the experience and he can go on to win the title one day."

Reflecting the ferocity of the fight Benn had to check himself into a London clinic during the night after blood was found in his urine. Years later in his autobiography Benn said, "Wharton was one of my toughest fights. Not necessarily the hardest, but certainly the toughest. Although I beat him on points and retained my title, I'd never came out of a ring as bruised as I did after that fight. My kidneys were quite badly affected and I had to undergo hospital checks which, thankfully, quelled my fears, and found my kidneys to be 100% OK. I'd been whacked in the kidneys before, but I'd never felt it like I did with Wharton."

While money was of secondary importance to Henry it cannot be denied it was his biggest pay-day by far. Terry O'Neill has maintained a detailed financial record of the fight. The purse was £365,000 (£615,000 in 2013). It wasn't divided up until all the expenses had been taken off the top. The cost of flights, sparring partners, hotel bills, food and other incidentals amounted to some £67,000 (£113,000). It isn't cheap to organise a lengthy training camp! The manager's share of 25%, split, of course, between Terry O'Neill and Mickey Duff came to around £75,000 (£126,000). The trainer's share, 10%, went also to Terry O'Neill, £30,000 (£50,000). This left Henry with around £195,000 (£328,000).

Sadly for all concerned some of these figures would become the subject of a legal discussion in the years to come.

CHAPTER 10

Change of Direction

An acrimonious parting of the ways seems to be a perennial feature at the top level of professional boxing. It usually involves a break up in relationships of people who have shared so much time together and been the closest of friends. Sadly, also, is the fact that money is inevitably involved somewhere along the line.

Gary Atkin, and his brothers, had been trained by Terry O'Neill at St Patricks gym since they'd been schoolboys. When people train at a gym for hours every week and travel to and from amateur boxing tournaments throughout the country, everyone gets to know each other very well. Family members become familiar, worries are shared and there is mutual respect. Henry Wharton joined this 'family' in his mid teens and shared those relationships.

Terry O'Neill, a deeply religious man, helped found the gym not long after the Second World War ended, and had become a respected trainer and official. As we know he'd taken the England team to the Commonwealth games in 1974 and until he became Henry's partial manager he was part of the English ABA selection committee. The gym had produced numerous schoolboy and amateur champions as well as inter-nationalists.

Throughout the five years Wharton had been a professional, Atkin and O'Neill were by his side, training with him, in his

corner for his fights and at the extended camp in preparation for
the Benn contest. They'd been through a lot together.

Shortly after the Benn fight Henry came to accept in his own
mind that a change was needed. Terry O'Neill had been a great
friend to him and been there every step of the way. His boxer's
contract was up for renewal and believed this was as good a time
as any to part company. One night, Henry travelled to the gym
with a heavy heart to advise Terry that it was time for both to
move on. Gary Atkin can remember seeing Henry going into
the office at the gym with Terry and both shaking hands when
their conversation was over. Henry hated doing this but felt it
was the only way to take himself to the next level.

Around this time Terry O'Neill remembers Mickey Duff
contacting him to discuss paying Atkin for his work in
preparation for the Benn fight. Terry agreed in principle, but
Duff argued that, as he (Atkin) was part of the training team,
then any fee due should come out of the 10% trainers fee. Before
going to America Henry had asked Akin to come with him and
Terry, and although initially reluctant due to the effect it would
have on his business, he eventually agreed. During their time in
both America and Spain Henry kept enquiring with Atkin if
anything had been resolved around him getting some sort of fee
for his assistance.

From Gary Atkin's point of view, he'd been off work for
virtually three months and had a home and new wife to support.
He'd ran and exercised with Henry every step of the way and
dipped into his own pocket for anything he'd needed. He didn't
ask for anything, but he did expect to be recompensed in the
fullness of time.

With Henry keen to get back to work he made the decision to ask Gary to be his new trainer. It was obviously an awkward situation for everyone involved and it would have been totally inappropriate to continue to use St Patricks gym as a training base.

Atkins' best man, Clint Tranmer, was the landlord of a large public house/night club in Leeds called the Compton Arms. There was a small amateur boxing club who used to train in the basement and at ground level was a nightclub known as Rocky's. Although the basement was a bit tight the night club only opened on Thursday, Friday and Saturday so on the other days there was facilities to erect a ring and hang punch bags. With the music from the club Henry and Gary got back into a routine and very quickly thereafter they were joined by other local boxers.

Some months later Atkin realised that he wasn't going to be financially rewarded for the time training Henry for the Benn fight, and sought advice from a local solicitor. The lawyer felt Atkin had a case, and legal proceedings followed. The matter was eventually settled out of court some years later. Not the happiest of circumstances for anyone, and to this day probably all regret what happened.

Henry, and Mickey Duff, were keen to get another fight arranged. Both felt that if Henry could get a few wins under his belt then a re-match would be made with Benn. Wharton was still frustrated at 'blowing' the first four rounds of their fight and was beginning to accept that perhaps the big occasion got to him. The idea of a possible re-match fitted neatly into place, when his next fight was on the undercard of Benn's title defence against Juan Giminez.

The big fight bill on 10 September took place at the National Exhibition Centre in Birmingham. Although the Benn fight was the main attraction, and Wharton would bring his usual band of supporters, probably the biggest selling fight of the night was the British light middle weight contest between the holder Rob McCracken and Steve Foster, both of whom had a large and vociferous following. This rivalry would have a bearing on Wharton's bout.

Henry's opponent, in an eight rounder, was an American from Tennessee, Guy Stanford. Stanford moved up and down between super middleweight and light heavy, winning in Tennessee and losing everywhere else. He'd fourteen wins and a draw at home before five defeats on the road. He was durable though, having been stopped only once.

Training went well and Gary Atkin was settling into his position as sole trainer. Marvin O'Brien and Darren Ashton were brought in for sparring, and occasionally Derek Roche, to bring Henry up to full sharpness.

Stanford was a tough opponent but Wharton was quickly on top. In the third round Henry can remember feeling that he was about to 'go' and the American was already cut around the eye. However, Henry became aware that a riot had started in the arena, between fans of McCracken and Foster. While his fight was in progress Henry was thinking that if the trouble continues the referee might halt the fight until it was brought under control. Realising that this would have given Stanford time to recover Wharton stormed forward throwing caution to the wind. A successful strategy as it turned out, because he over-powered the American and brought the fight to an end in jig time.

With Benn also winning and retaining his title the possibility of a return with Wharton was high on the agenda, but as the weeks moved on and no definite decisions were being made Mickey Duff had to look elsewhere. Wharton was still the Commonwealth champion and was being pressed to defend his crown. But while Henry had returned to training immediately after the Stanford fight he'd no firm idea of who his next opponent would be.

Trainer and friend Gary Atkin can recall clearly how this situation took a dramatic and unexpected turn. "We were in the gym at Rocky's Bar, Henry was bandaged up and there was only me and him in the gym. He was shadow boxing and my phone went. It was Mickey and he says, 'Are you with Henry? I need to make a decision. We've been offered a fight with Eubank, but I'll tell you now – I don't like it. What does Henry think?'. I shouts across to Henry, 'If you want to take a little longer to think about it, but Mickey's got a chance with Eubank, do you want it?'. He didn't even take a breath, he just looked across and nodded. I told Mickey he wanted the fight and Mickey said, 'Remember, I don't like the fight, I think he's the wrong opponent'.

So it was as simple as that. A world title fight against Chris Eubank, the WBO champion, who was on an incredible series of world title fights in a short space of time, was on, with a brief nod of the head. The reasons why Henry was so quick to accept the fight were relatively simple. Firstly, it was another opportunity to fight for a world title so quickly after the Benn challenge, and secondly, he was convinced he'd the style to beat Eubank.

The official announcement for the fight was arranged for the Waldorf Hotel in London on 26 September, and Gary Atkin and the owner of the Compton Arms, Clint Tranmer, wasted no time in making arrangements. They hired a white stretch limo, chauffeur as well, to take Henry and other friends all the way from Leeds down to London. It was a great laugh for all concerned, but it sent a message as well – we're in the big time now! The fight was scheduled for the G-Mex Centre in Manchester.

One of the reasons Henry had moved on from Terry O'Neill was that he felt he needed something different in terms of being coached. Mickey Duff knew this, as did Gary Atkin. Atkin could get Henry fit, and he had coaching skills as well, gathered over many years in and around good boxers, and trainers, in the Leeds area, but at world level he was still learning the ropes. With this in mind, and after consulting Henry and Gary, Duff brought in Saoul Mamby from New York.

Mamby had been an exceptionally talented boxer, being stopped only once in a twenty nine year professional career in which he'd fought the best in the world at light welterweight and welterweight. He'd fought in Vietnam during the war and turned to boxing in 1969 after visiting Jamaica. Mamby won the WBC light welter title in 1980, making five successful defences. Included in his list of opponents was Roberto Duran to whom he'd lost on points. Coincidentally he'd also twice fought former Wharton amateur opponent, Glenwood Brown, indeed he was still fighting when he was brought over to England to train Henry at the age of forty seven!

Wharton described the experience of working with Mamby being similar to opening a new book for the first time. He was learning something on each page, and he couldn't wait to turn over to the next. Mamby knew so much, and Henry was benefiting from that vast level of knowledge. Wharton's attitude to boxing was always positive. If he caught a hard punch, he didn't get despondent – he wanted to learn where he had gone wrong, so working with Mamby was right up his street. He thoroughly enjoyed going to the gym each day with Mamby and when he was having a move explained to him Wharton would smile 'from ear to ear,' such was his enjoyment at learning something new.

Gary Atkin can certainly recall one unusual procedure he picked up from Mamby. For years Wharton had been struggling to make the 12st limit for title fights. Mamby knew this, and suggested they have Henry steep in a warm bath with dissolved molasses and rock salt. Atkin set off to the local supermarket in search of molasses, not having a clue what they were. Neither did anyone at the supermarket. However an elderly lady was listening in to the conversation and she said that it was simply treacle. So Gary bought something akin to 'Golden Syrup' and Henry started having baths in this solution. Whether it was psychological or not, Wharton did lose weight easier and felt refreshed the following morning, believing that while the pores were opening to let the sweat out, they were also letting in sugar from the syrup and the salt.

Although the Eubank fight had been finalised, both of them were committed to prior title defences, and potential banana skins. Eubank's bout in South Africa on 15 October against Dan Schommer was far riskier than Wharton's Commonwealth match up with Zimbabwean, Sipho Moyo, eleven days later.

Eubank did retain his crown on a unanimous decision but it caused widespread controversy. The British champion was lacklustre and most experts thought he'd lost. It'd been Eubank's fifth world title defence in eight months, an unheard of schedule in modern times.

On 26 October in Leeds Town Hall, Wharton, with Saoul Mamby in his corner, had to win to hold up his end of the bargain. To be frank Moyo should never have been anywhere near a fight with someone of Wharton's pedigree, as he was preparing for a second world title clash. Moyo had ten wins from eleven fights, all in Zimbabwe, and had beaten no one whom anyone would have recognised.

As it turned out the highlight of evening was the unexpected appearance of Eubank and his promoter, Barry Hearn, high up in the balcony of the Town Hall, to the anticipated cat-calls and abuse from Wharton's fans. By that time Moyo had been counted out, after being flattened with a body shot in the very first round. Gary Atkin remembered thinking how brave, or stupid, Eubank was to be standing up on the balcony with his cane, preening himself, with around 1,200 Travellers baying for his blood. Eubank never flinched, he just kept on staring down at the crowd like a Caesar in Rome. Great publicity from a real showman.

Almost immediately after the fight, and without any prior warning, Mamby disappeared back to America. He'd been staying at the Clock Hotel in Leeds which at that time was a simple bed and breakfast place. He was very quite and he couldn't have been enjoying the experience in a strange country where he knew nobody. Duff had made the arrangements with

the cost coming off the top of Wharton's purse for the Eubank
fight. There might have been discussions between Henry's
manager and Mamby after the Moyo fight, but the boxer himself
wasn't aware of them. Wharton can recall Mamby telling him
that Eubank wouldn't like Mamby being by his side in the build
up to the fight, because Eubank knew that Mamby had been
with him in his early days in New York. Mamby thought this
fact would spook the champion. With Mamby saying this,
Wharton fully expected him to stay around until the fight had
taken place. We will never know now if Mamby's theory would
have came to fruition.

On 31 October the official press conference was held in the
Lancaster Suite of the Midland Hotel in Manchester, with both
boxers posing for cameras on the steps outside. Wharton's purse
was announced as being £100,000, less than a third of that for
the Benn fight. At the conference Wharton was very excited at
the prospect of having a second attempt at a world title. He was
confident of winning. He felt all the pieces of the jigsaw were
coming together at just the right time. He still believed Saoul
Mamby would be in his corner, he felt fit, was happy with his
training facilities and he knew he'd improved, mentally, since
the Benn fight. This caused him to speak directly to Eubank,
something he always tried to avoid. Wharton said, "Chris I
thought you were a clever guy. Why, if you could have picked
anybody, why in the world did you pick me. I just can't believe
that you'd want to fight me." Henry was trying to get a reaction,
and failed miserably. Eubank had seen it all before.

In early November Henry and Gary set off to Tenerife to set
up a three week training camp. They were accommodated at the

Garden City Olympus Club in Las Americas, in premises owned by a personal friend of Atkin, Hedley Rhodes, who sadly passed away in May 2013. They also managed to get full use of Nigel Benn's gym at nearby Royal Sunset Beach Club, an arrangement made between Gary and Peter DeFreitas in a hotel at the NEC after the Benn/Giminez and Wharton/Stanford fights.

This time however the sparring started sooner than expected! There was a pub/restaurant at the complex called the Winning Post and on their first night on the island Wharton and Atkin decided to go for a drink before the tough training regime got under way. Gary Atkin tells the story. "There were three Welsh kids, big lads, and we were talking and they were all right at first. But we'd been drinking and one of them was just getting a bit mouthy. He was starting to criticise Henry and I could see in his face he wanted to kill this kid. Now Henry was always friendly when people came up to speak to him he always took time to chat with them, but I just knew this guy was going too far. So I said 'lets go' and he just stood there with his pint and said, 'let me finish this.' I said ,'well I'm off to the toilet, keep calm Henry'. So I'm off to the toilet which was at the end of a short corridor. When I came out all I could hear was tables and glasses falling all over the place and when I got back into the bar all three Welsh lads were scattered everywhere. I got a hold of Henry and said, 'get out of here'. But they had started to get obnoxious, and I think they'd been at some kick boxing tournament on Tenerife and Henry thought they were taking the piss."

Each morning around 6am, Wharton and Atkin would drive up to the plateau of Mount Tiede, approximately 8,000 feet,

Courtesy of Nigel Holland, photographer.

15: This time the photographer's in the photo! Henry with Nigel Holland.

This page: 16: Henry with Saoul Mamby, brought into camp by Mickey Duff. *17:* Arriving in style. All the way from Leeds to London to announce the Eubank fight. *Facing page: 18:* Press conference for the Eubank fight. Atkin, Wharton, Barry Hearn and Eubank. *19:* Eubank ducks below a Wharton right hander.

18

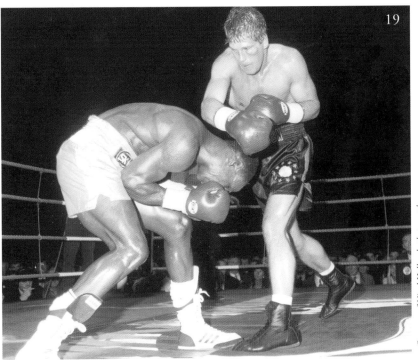

19

This page: 20: Wharton with Commonwealth and European belts after beating Sam Storey. *Facing page: 21:* Henry with Robin Reid holding the WBC belt. *22:* Frank Warren and Mickey Duff shaking on pre-fight £50,000 bet.

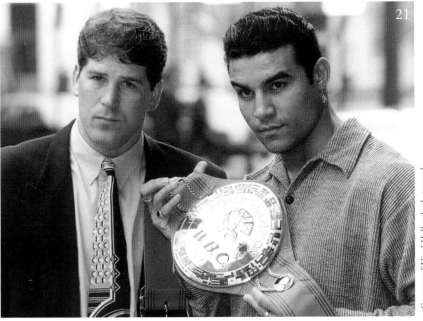

Courtesy of Nigel Holland, photographer.

Frank Warren

Henry Wharton

Courtesy of Nigel Holland, photographer.

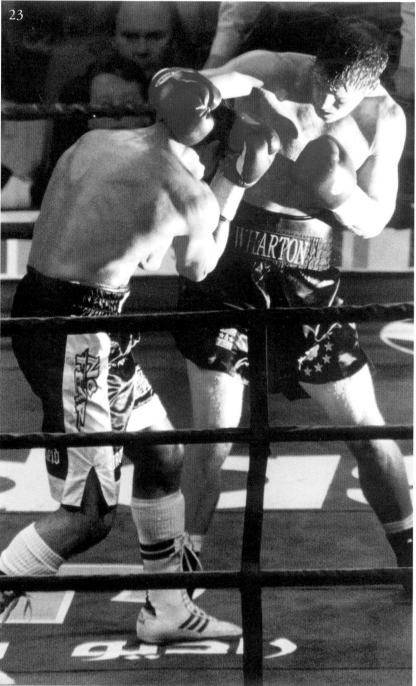

Previous page: 23: Action from the Robin Reid fight.
This page: 24: The Wharton clan, Lyla, Billy, Jersey, Amanda,
Maddison, Henry, Sonny and Oscar. *Following page: 25:* A young
Wharton as a pro, but still wearing his England amateur badge on
his shorts.

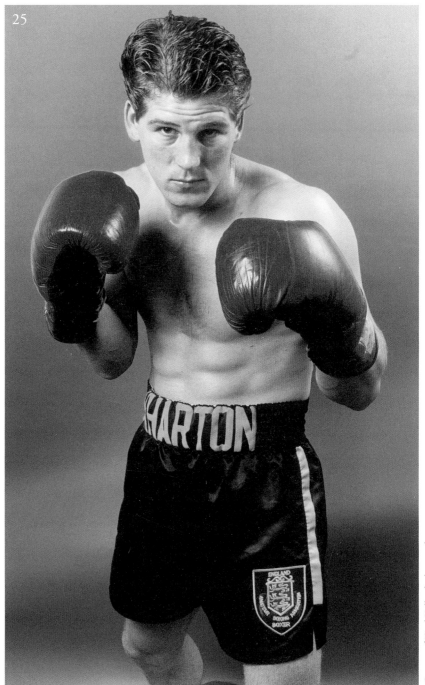

and run for an hour. Other boxers have done the same type of training at this high altitude and many tourists who've visited this area will have experienced the sense of breathlessness just from walking about. However, neither Wharton nor Atkin were affected in any way, indeed the only thing unusual about their training was a surprising inability to break sweat. It was only when they were driving back down off the mountain that the perspiration started.

Mickey Duff had arranged good quality sparring for Henry and joining the team in Tenerife were Bobbie Joe Edwards, Mark Baker and Lester Jacobs. Edwards was a solid light heavyweight, Jacobs was unbeaten in eleven fights and Baker had eleven wins from twelve. Funnily enough Edwards' last fight before heading for Tenerife was against Henry's former gym mate, Michael Gale.

Accidents do happen when sparring, and on one occasion a left hook from Henry caught Lester Jacobs causing him to bite through his gumshield. An injury which needed eight stitches to repair. Jacobs was not upset in the slightest because he was contracted for a set period and being paid regardless of whether he was fit to spar or not. Henry still has a smile to himself to this day, as he remembers walking past Jacobs to the gym each morning, being toasted by the injured boxer sipping a Pina Colada while enjoying the sunshine. Sadly for Lester however his view of Tenerife was to become somewhat blurry!

Mickey Duff, as was his habit, decided to visit Tenerife to check on the progress of his world title challenger. As Atkin explained, Duff was a real life jet-setter, and workaholic. He was so busy travelling all over the world to make deals that he used the flights to sleep and recover. This sometimes left him disorientated which, when he found himself in Tenerife, would have painful consequences.

Duff arrived at the wrong complex in Las Americas and hailed a taxi to transport him the short distance to the Garden City apartments. The taxi driver asked for 150 pesetas, a cheap fare, and the going rate. However, Mickey was still thinking in US currency and thought the taxi driver was charging him $150. The elderly promoter was not one to lie down when he believed he was being ripped off and ended up in a fight with the taxi driver. When he appeared at Wharton's apartment his face was bleeding and his glasses were smashed. Of course Mickey couldn't see a thing and the only person who had spectacles was Lester Jacobs, and he wore those large round glasses favoured by African-Americans in the 1970s. For the next couple of days the real challenge for Henry and the sparring partners was to keep their faces straight when Mickey Duff was walking around wearing Jacob's spectacles!

When they got back to England and the build up was starting in earnest, the press were reporting that Mickey Duff wanted to pick the judges. Duff's opinion was that Eubank had lost the Schommer fight in South Africa and wanted to ensure that top quality judges would be on duty. Of course this was partly a publicity stunt, but he did get what he wanted when two of the judges appointed were British, Paul Thomas and Roy Francis along with Gerald Maltz from the States. The referee was the highly experienced American, Steve Smoger.

Duff wasn't yet finished with his antics. The final press conference and weigh-in were held at the Portland Thistle Hotel in Manchester on the day before the fight. According to Wharton everything had gone well in the build up. There were no injuries, the weight had eventually came off, sparring had been brilliant and everybody in the camp, including Henry, were confident that he'd win.

Then at the press conference came an incredible outburst from Mickey Duff. Out of the blue he called Eubank 'scum'. Wharton had been aware of a couple of comments Duff had made about Eubank which tended to indicate there was some personal dislike, but this was totally unexpected. Henry likens Duff's actions as being equivalent to swearing in church. As he recalls, "I was thinking, where has that come from. The hairs are standing on the back of my hand today when I think about it. Why would he say that about another boxer at a press conference. The world's media were sat in front of us and he called Chris 'scum'. I was speechless, if someone had asked me a question I couldn't have got a word out. I remember it like it was yesterday. I was in a trance, I couldn't believe it. Even though he was my manager, I couldn't back him. It was just so outrageous. Chris just stood and said something but I could see he was angry. Put it this way, if Mickey had been younger they'd have came to blows. Instead of the usual carry on with someone coming between the fighters, I actually came between Chris and Mickey!"

It was a confident Wharton camp as the final preparations wound down for the Eubank fight.

CHAPTER 11

Eubank Fight

In 1994 it would be fair to say that Chris Eubank was not a popular figure in British boxing. He wasn't even a popular figure with the general public, who'd come to know him through his extroverted ways. His eye-glass, cane, jodhpurs, tweed jacket and eloquent use of the English language had set himself up as an eccentric, but more often than not, he was seen as an arrogant fool.

We must remember that in the beginning, Cassius Clay/Muhammad Ali, was widely disliked. His stance on Vietnam brought him into conflict with white-collar Americans and his boastfulness upset many traditional boxing commentators. Ali came to be revered throughout the world, and although Eubank hasn't achieved that type of fame, time has allowed followers of boxing to become more appreciative of his immense boxing ability and to look more sympathetically at his character.

He was a publicists hero. He could draw a crowd, any place, anywhere and at any time. Was it an act, or was this the real man?

He'd had a troubled upbringing which led him into an early life of street crime. Ending up in New York, he became a professional boxer before returning to Britain. Between 1985 and 1987 his first five bouts in Atlantic City all resulted in points victories. It was over a year before he fought again, this time at Effingham Country Club in Sussex. Over the next two years his stock gradually rose with fourteen straight wins, ten inside the distance. His wins over Anthony Logan, Johnny Melfah and Denys Cronin confirmed that he was heading in the right direction.

Between March and September 1990 he won, and twice defended, the lightly regarded WBC International middleweight title, but the big breakthrough came on 18 November that year when he stopped Nigel Benn in the ninth round to annex the WBO middleweight crown. Over the next twelve months he made three successful defences before stepping up to super middleweight to beat Michael Watson in the last round, resulting in the tragic circumstances faced by the loser.

In modern boxing, world champions usually engage in a maximum of three title fights per year. There are a variety of reasons for this, including tax issues and the physical demands of peaking for each fight. In 1992 Eubank made no less than five successful defences in England, Portugal and Scotland. Chris took it easy the following year! After two defences, he put his title on the line in a rematch with Nigel Benn who now held the WBC version. Their fight ended in a draw.

When he took to the ring on 10 December against Wharton, he'd already defended the WBO title five times, in Germany, Northern Ireland, England, Wales and South Africa. He was a world champion in the truest sense of the word.

When Eubank had his last fight in 1998 he weighed 13st 7lb and his body looked no different to what it did when he fought at the 12st limit. He was immensely strong as a super middleweight and was always in top condition. He was extremely confident and that allowed him to be relaxed in the ring. This meant he was very quick to react, either to avoid punches or to let them go. He was not a 'one punch' knockout artist, but he could punch very hard indeed. His chin was like iron and in fifty two fights against the biggest hitters around he was stopped only once, his last fight, at cruiserweight. When legendary British boxers are being discussed, Chris Eubank can't be excluded.

This then was the man Wharton was facing in Manchester. It has to be said that very often in his title defences, Eubank would fight only in spurts, and on reflection this happened against lesser opponents. He would throw a flurry of punches, impress the judges and make his opponent wary of going on the offensive. All the while Eubank would be shuffling about the ring, posing really, but more importantly conserving his energy. Henry, and others, had seen this, and the Yorkshire man knew that he was fit enough to press a fight for the entire twelve rounds. This is why Wharton was so confident going into the fight. He felt he could force Eubank into a brawl and possibly get to him in the later rounds.

The packed G-Mex Centre, with 10,000 fans inside, was rocking when the boxers were introduced. It was later estimated that 8,000 of those were Wharton supporters. Henry, with Mickey Duff, Gary Atkin and Dennie Mancini in his corner looked eager to get started and as usual Eubank was posing like a peacock, apparently unconcerned. Wharton came out with his game plan to put pressure on the champion from the very first second, but was met by a man who was back to his brilliant best. Eubank was on his toes and jabbing to perfection. Henry clearly

was not overawed, as perhaps he was at the beginning of the
Benn fight, but was being hit often, and lost the first round.

The second was a superb session for the fans. Eubank
continued jabbing to perfection and now stepping in with heavy
shots. Wharton was making Eubank work but he suffered a
swelling under his left eye following a right cross from the
champion. Another round to Eubank. The tide turned a little
in the third, when midway through, a long right hand from
Wharton seemed to disturb Eubank. There were signs of the
pace getting to Eubank as he gulped for air and this may have
been a round won by the challenger.

The fourth was another tough one for both boxers, but
Eubank was looking impressive. Several big punches from
Eubank got through and he won the round clearly. In the next
Wharton piled forward and had some success with left hooks
and at times Eubank looked to be fading. There was a strong case
to suggest Wharton took this round. There can be no doubt that
the sixth belonged to Henry. He chased a retreating Eubank
from corner to corner concentrating on left hooks to do the job.
At this stage in the fight it was easy to score certain rounds to
Eubank because he won them convincingly, the first, second
and fourth being examples. The other three rounds were hard
to ajudicate but Wharton could have taken them depending on
how an independent observer might assess them.

The fight swung completely towards Eubank during the next
three rounds. The seventh was noticeably slower than the rest
but Eubank landed the cleaner punches. In the eighth Eubank
fought like a man possessed forcing Wharton onto the ropes and
letting huge shots go. At the beginning of the ninth Eubank

unleashed a barrage of punches and chased Henry along the ropes. At one point Eubank tried the old Ali trick of motioning the referee in to stop the fight in the interests of protecting the stricken fighter, but Wharton laughed and Steve Smoger ignored the bravado.

In the tenth Eubank gave Henry a boxing lesson. He skipped round the outside of the ring firing out stinging jabs, landing regularly on Wharton's injured eye. Henry simply followed Eubank without getting close enough to land any worthwhile punches. Before the start of the penultimate round Dennie Mancini could be seen squeezing Wharton's eye with the metal 'endswell' in a desperate effort to keep the eye open. Typically for Wharton, he never knew when he was beaten, and rose at the bell determined to turn the fight his way. He battled through the round landing good shots on the tiring Eubank. Before the start of the last round the doctor had been asked to examine Wharton's eye but he failed miserably in the attempt as Duff and Mancini argued with him until he was forced to give up.

When the final bell rang Henry knew he still had a 'punchers chance' and gave it everything. An exhausted Eubank tottered round the ring trying to avoid the Wharton onslaught and succeeded for most of the three minutes. At the bell there was no doubt who'd won. When the scorecards were read out Roy Francis had it 118 – 112 (or eight rounds to Eubank, two to Wharton and two even). Gerald Maltz scored it 116 – 112 (eight rounds to Eubank, four to Wharton) and Paul Thomas's original scorecard had it 114 – 113, but was later corrected to 115 – 113 (seven rounds to Eubank and five to Wharton).

In Eubank's autobiography he reports that it was an

'incredibly tough fight'. His analysis of proceedings were that, 'he(Wharton) used his great strength and persisted, persisted, persisted. However, with the benefit of hindsight, Wharton came into the fight with almost too much heart, because I worked around that and used my technical skills to defeat him. If he had pulled back a little, reviewed the terrain, strategized perhaps, he may have had the beating of me.'

Eubank's trainer Ronnie Davies felt that his performance against Wharton was one of the three best of his career. Eubank on further reflection felt, 'that the contest was so hard, that it almost broke my spirit. After the fight there was a press conference in which I sighed deeply, saying, 'I can't do this anymore'.

In his book Eubank also explained why the fight was so tough. 'The reason I felt so jaded was the effect on me of Wharton's resolve, his heart. Yes, I had won the fight and it was a spectacular performance. However, when you hit a guy so heavily and repeatedly but he just keeps coming, it eventually breaks your morale. I couldn't stop Wharton, he was like a choo-choo train, huffing and puffing, he just wouldn't stop coming forward. Before the fight, I had given him a six for technical ability which was accurate, but he was easily a ten for persistence. His spirit was unstoppable.' Three months later Eubank lost to Steve Collins, his first defeat in forty four fights. Did Henry take something from Eubank that night?

The memory of the fight remains vivid for Wharton. "It was a classic. I watch it back on DVD and it was, it was a classic. I still think- what a fight. For how well he performed, I tried too. He had to put that performance in because I never stopped. It was endless for me. Early on in the fight he hit me with a right hand but my left eye was swelling up from almost the start and I couldn't really see his shots coming. Chris threw a funny left hand and it almost seemed to guard the right hand and you couldn't see it coming until the last second. I used to have a decent eye for seeing punches coming, but I couldn't see his coming. From about the fourth round onwards my vision was blurred, I couldn't see the right hands coming and I couldn't get out the way. If you imagine putting a glass down on a table and closing one eye, when you try to pick it up you sometimes miss it. That's what I was like, but it was worse because I was trying to avoid a moving target. If my eye had been OK, I felt the fight was close, certainly not as far away as one judge had it, I'd have made more right hands miss, and I would have landed more, because not only did it effect me not seeing his right hands coming, I couldn't land properly, I was missing by miles on occasion. As a professional boxer, someone whose paid for what they do, to practice endlessly, to miss by those margins shows something was wrong. In all my career I'd never thrown as many right hands and missed by so much a distance. I couldn't work it out at the time."

Wharton had known that this was going to be a tough, long drawn out fight and he knew that he'd be fit enough to push it for the full twelve rounds. As previous fights with Smith and Benn had shown, Wharton would still be driving forward when the opposition were tiring fast. This was how Henry thought the fight would go with Eubank. In this fight however, Henry acknowledges that Eubank didn't tire. He was superbly fit, as Henry says, 'he was bouncing, he was jumping out his skin.'

It is interesting to learn of the quandary Wharton was in prior to the Eubank fight.

He knew he'd thrown away the first four rounds with Benn by standing off him, and afterwards he vowed to himself that if he ever got another world title chance he wouldn't make the same mistake. On the other hand, he realised that Eubank's strength was that he was a counter-puncher, someone who waits for the opponent to come forward, making him miss, and then striking. So Henry went into the fight knowing that by attacking he was playing into Eubank's hands. Nevertheless, he felt that the way to win the fight was to make him work for every second, drain his stamina, and wear him down towards the end.

As the fight was progressing, and the injury began to affect his vision, it was perhaps his corner's duty to advise Wharton to try something different. As Henry explained previously during a discussion with Mickey Duff following the Benn fight, a boxer can get into a rhythm, either a slow or fast pace, and they can't get out of it. In this occasion Henry was in 'all out attack' mode, and nobody could've changed it. Even if Gary Atkin, or Mickey Duff, had been screaming at him, it would have made no difference.

When Henry got home and settled down after the fight he had to realise that he'd failed for a second time to achieve his lifetime's ambition and fulfil his dad Billy's prediction. The eye injury would heal and the aches and pains subside but how would he cope mentally? He was 27 years old, been British and Commonwealth champion, he'd earned good money and was a minor celebrity in North Yorkshire. He'd been training, almost without a break, since he was a young teenager, and his only outlet, perhaps unusually for a boxer, seemed to be in his golf. He certainly didn't want to become a financially lucrative stepping stone for younger fighters, nor did he believe he'd been brought down to that level because he'd lost to two exceptional, world class boxers. Indeed, given another chance at either, he felt he could beat them.

This is how Wharton remembers his feelings at that point. "The Eubank fight was a real, tough defeat for me. The Benn one was, like, these things happen, you learn, you come back and you win. But the Eubank fight was like, I really tried hard, and I can confess now that I broke something in me that night. I tried so hard and the punishment I took, I don't think I was ever the same fighter again. Something happened to me that night, I burst a few strings, my body was never the same. I had ran harder than I'd ever ran before, I'd taken more punishment that I'd ever taken before, and I'd tried so hard to win that some strings in my bow had snapped. I was questioning myself – can I do this? Am I good enough to be the champion of the world? This was the first time in my life I had thought this. I never thought of giving up boxing but I was asking what was going to happen now. I was sitting with someone one day, I don't remember who it was, and this chap said, 'what are you going to do now then?' He was being sympathetic towards me and I said, 'what do you mean?' He obviously had doubts and it was like lighting a match inside me. I suddenly got it back. I told him 'I'll tell you what I'm going to do. I'm going to reclaim the number one spot, and I'm going to fight for the world title and I'm going to win it.' And that was me, I was back. The self doubt was gone."

The old fighting instinct had returned, and after a few months he was back in the gym looking for his next contest.

CHAPTER 12

European champion

At the start of 1995 when Wharton was beginning to get over the Eubank defeat he'd been replaced by Frenchman, Frederic Seillier, as the number one contender to Nigel Benn's WBC crown. A match with Benn was the main target for Mickey Duff and Seillier, who was also the European champion, seemed to be the main obstacle.

Jimmy Greaves once said that football was a 'funny old game', but boxing can surpass that adage. It became known that Benn was committed to a huge title fight against the awesome American, Gerald McClellan, in February, and Seillier, possibly seeing his world title chance slipping into the distance, decided to make an attempt on the WBA version in May, vacating the European title in the process.

This opened up twin opportunities for Duff, and the shrewd old manager grabbed them with both hands. He managed to persuade the European Boxing Union to accept Henry as an opponent for Italian, Mauro Galvano, in a contest for the vacant championship. Duff knew that victory for Wharton would not only secure another title but install him, once again, as the number one contender for Benn's crown.

When Duff contacted Wharton and told him about the Galvano fight he warned him that they might have to go to Italy. Henry was game for that idea because he loved travelling to different countries, but Duff told him 'you don't want to go to Italy, son!' Anyway, purse bids were submitted, eventually won by Duff with a figure of £100,000 according to press reports. The fight was arranged for 8 July at the Barbican in York.

Right from the moment the fight was announced Henry got the impression that Duff was concerned. When he visited Leeds to watch Henry working out he would make comments like, 'styles make fights' and 'Galvano's a tall lad' and 'he's awkward' and all these types of comments were giving Wharton the impression that his manager had doubts he'd win.

Making the weight had become a major problem for Wharton and for each title fight it was becoming the number one area of concern. Looking back now it's clear his body had simply outgrown the super middleweight limit. When someone for weeks on end is running five or six miles every morning, training flat out two or three times a day, avoiding all fatty foods and with only a week or so before a fight, still can't get within fourteen pounds of the weight, then they've a problem! Mickey Duff was aware of the issue and made remarks in the press about Henry moving up to light heavyweight. Indeed Duff had suggested that he'd contacted representatives of the French based WBC champion at that weight, Christophe Tiozzo, with a view to arranging a match.

On the day of the weigh in, Henry's mother Janet, couldn't bear to look at her son, he was so pale. Before it was due to take place Wharton, in a full sweat suit was skipping as hard as he could, and jumping in and out of a sauna trying to lose the last few pounds. He couldn't take a shower because the water might seep into the pores putting weight back on, so his trainer would dry him with a rough towel believing that rubbing some skin off might make a difference. Fortunately for Henry, he just made the weight yet again.

When the weigh in was over Wharton went with Atkin and a friend, Sean Daly, to an Italian restaurant in York, Silvanos. After two mouthfulls of spaghetti Henry had to rush to the toilet to be sick, his stomach obviously reacting to the food. He thought he was going to pass out as the sweat came out on him. The feeling passed however and he demolished a couple of pints of beer in the restaurant. After a few hours Henry and Sean walked through the town stopping at pubs and had another few pints! Wharton reckons that he might have drank eight or nine pints that day before having another meal later in the evening. By bedtime he was beginning to feel human again, but hardly ideal preparation for a European title fight!

Galvano was a top notch opponent. Stopped only once in his career by Nigel Benn. He defeated Londoner, Mark Kaylor, for the European title in March 1990 and nine months later became the WBC champion beating Dario Matteoni. Over the next two years he defended his world title twice, beating Ron Essett and Juan Ferreyra before running into Benn. In March 1993 in a re-match he lost again, this time on points. In November that year fellow Italian, Vincenzo Nardiello, beat him on points for his old European title. In all, he'd taken part in thirty four fights, winning twenty eight, losing five, with one draw. He was a clever boxer, taller than most of Wharton's opponents, but with only eight inside the distance victories, not a big puncher.

When Mike Goodall made the pre-fight announcements, sitting proudly at ringside, as a special guest, was young

Wharton fan from Leeds, and kidney transplant recipient, Craig Marshall. Wharton quickly got the Barbican crowd on their feet with a storming first three minutes. He landed every punch in the book as Galvano circled the ring going backwards trying to avoid the blows coming his way. When the bell rang it looked like it was going to be an early night. In the next round Galvano obviously realised that he'd need to return some punches or Wharton would run over the top of him and he did have some success, landing the cleaner blows. The Italian did however suffer for his determination when he was cut on his left eyelid. This round was probably a draw.

In the third, Henry seemed to lose his way. He was much slower and missing wildly. Galvano perhaps believed the tide had turned and was coming forward more, landing regularly and jolting Wharton's head back. The Italian clearly won that round.

It looked like more of the same as the fourth round progressed, but suddenly Henry landed a vicious left hook while in close and it detonated on Galvano's nose, knocking the Italian down and out. As German referee Heinrich Muhmert finished his count, poor Galvano's face was a bloody mess. Wharton spat out his gumshield and kicked it into the crowd. He was back with a bang and added the European belt to his Commonwealth bauble. Although Wharton had put the Eubank defeat behind him this result was nevertheless a relief. "I remember afterwards there was something inside, like a defiance saying, 'who said I was finished,' but it was me who was saying it. Nobody else said it. I had it figured in my own mind that people were saying it about me. I kept shouting it and I said to Mickey Duff, 'I'm finished am I?' and he went, 'I never said you were finished', and I said, 'yes you did' and we were arguing and afterwards when we got back to the dressing rooms I said, 'you didn't like that Mickey did you, you thought I was finished', and he kept repeating that he'd never said that. I said, 'you never thought I'd beat him, did you?' but I was as high as a kite. Eventually I said, 'sorry Mickey, I've built this picture up myself.' ".

Also on the bill that night were Henry's friends and stable mates, Ron Hopley and Denzil Browne, although former team mate at St Pat's, Michael Gale, missed out through injury. Interestingly enough Joe Calzaghe was on the show, beating Tyrone Jackson in four rounds. Gary Atkin can remember both Joe and his father Enzo, preferring their own company in the changing rooms and didn't seem to want to mix with the other trainers and boxers.

The Wharton camp had a minor scare in the days following the fight. The EBU required their title contenders to submit to drug tests after their fights and Sports Council officials should have been in attendance for that purpose. These arrangements should have been made by the British Boxing Board of Control who later admitted their failure to do this. Once back home, the Italian camp began to make noises about the title being declared vacant and having a re-match ordered. This request, thankfully, fell on deaf ears.

A short break was due, and Henry indulged in his new golfing passion, even managing to win a local amateur trophy, but Duff, and to be fair Wharton himself, were keen to keep the kettle boiling. The win over Galvano kept him high in the world rankings and with weight making a major concern it was important not to allow too great a period between training camps. With Eubank having lost his world title, and Benn committed to other defences, all Wharton had to do was to keep winning.

In September Duff proposed a fight with Northern Irishman, Sam Storey, in defence of the European crown. Henry was keen on the idea for a number of reasons, but foremost among these was his belief that Storey held the British title. The beautifully crafted Lonsdale Belt given to British champions, and kept for ever if they won three title fights, is much coveted among British boxers, and Henry was no exception. Of course he'd one British title victory in the bag when he'd beaten Fidel Smith in 1992, and always hoped to do enough before retiring to win the belt outright.

On 5 October, when turning up late at the Queens Hotel in Leeds for the press conference to announce the fight, he still had it in mind that the bout would be for his European and Commonwealth championships and Storey's British title. Storey had won that belt in April, beating Ali Forbes, and hadn't yet defended it. Wharton wasn't aware that Storey had given up the British title, and the vacant championship would be contested by Joe Calzaghe and Stephen Wilson at the end of that month.

Calzaghe, who at that time was also managed by Mickey Duff, states in his autobiography that his manager liked to do things in a traditional way and that meant fighting for the British title, then the European, before progressing to a charge at the world crown. In the book Joe says that Duff felt he was a better boxer than Wharton but that Henry was ahead of

Calzaghe in the queue and he'd have to wait his turn to progress.

It wouldn't be too much a stretch of the imagination to suggest that it would have been very beneficial for Duff, and his National Promotions set-up, to split the three titles. If Wharton and Calzaghe won, then Duff would control all three, and even if Storey won, he could have offered him a fight with Calzaghe in an attempt to win back his British title. The only thing was in all this, is that it seems Wharton hadn't been made aware of the master plan!

Research has now shown that Sam Storey sent a letter to the British Boxing Board, for their September meeting, relinquishing the British title. This was accepted, and he was advised that he'd be looked upon favourably should he wish to contest the title in the future. The Board then sanctioned a fight between Joe Calzaghe and Stephen Wilson for the vacant championship on the proviso that they agree in writing to defend, after a period of grace, against whoever they nominate. The alternative position could well have been that Calzaghe might have been Storey's mandatory defence, and the Board could possibly have refused to sanction a Wharton contest.

Neither Wharton nor Gary Atkin can recall the exact details of why Storey hadn't retained his British title, and to this day Henry is upset that the three belts weren't on the line. He can say for a fact he was never told directly by Duff that the British crown wasn't up for grabs, and indeed he recalls seeing an early poster or some type of publicity brochure with the British title being listed. Gary Atkin shed some light on how these type of things can happen. "I remember going down to London with Henry for a meeting with Mickey Duff in December 1997 and we went to a fight bill at Wembley. During the course of the night Clinton Woods and Mark Baker came into the ring and they announced that it was for the Commonwealth super middle weight title. I looked at Henry and he shrugged his shoulders in surprise because at that time we thought Henry still held it." We can recall too the circumstances when Henry relinquished the British title he won from Fidel Smith, it just seemed to 'happen', there was no formal agreement made between Duff, O'Neill and Wharton.

It's easy to understand why Duff might have wanted to separate the three titles given the real threat Storey posed to his future plans. The Belfast man was dangerous opposition for anyone at the time and his southpaw stance was simply another difficulty the opposition faced. When he met Wharton he'd been fighting for ten years. His first defeat had been against future world champion, Steve Collins, in Boston, but in 1989 he took the British title from Tony Burke. There was one successful defence when he stopped Noel Magee, but in October 1990 he lost it to the very capable James Cook. Storey worked his way back, and fought Chris Eubank for the WBO crown in 1994 but was stopped in the seventh. Then came his second British title reign in April when her beat Ali Forbes.

Atkin brought in specialist southpaw sparring in the shape of rising young star Ryan Rhodes from Brendan Ingle's gym, and unbeaten cruiserweight, Rob Norton. Rhodes being lighter and faster was used to get Henry's speed up, and Norton being heavier and taller would present Wharton with a style more like Storey's. Henry's friend, Denzil Browne, was always in the gym for additional sparring.

Nowadays when the public can watch championship level boxers standing nose to nose at the weigh in, calling each other names and making threats, it's astonishing to delve into Wharton's mindset as the Storey fight approached. "This was going to be a test because Sam Storey was a good fighter, a southpaw as well and a clever guy at that. A gentleman, a real nice guy and his family were good people. It was a fight I didn't really want. I mean he's such a nice guy, it was almost like his family were my family. But we obviously had to box, he wanted to win and I wanted to win." The modern approach to create animosity between the fighters in a belief that this is needed to generate interest and sell more tickets, is a sad facet of the modern game, and probably unnecessary.

The Storey fight was arranged for the Northbridge Leisure Centre in Halifax on 11 November. Henry had never fought there before as a professional, but it did have an 1,800 capacity and was near enough Wharton's fan base. Clearly Leeds Town Hall and the Barbican in York must have been unavailable.

Once again weight making was an horrendous problem. Wharton maintains that he's seen TV coverage of himself and Storey being interviewed in the dressing rooms before the fight and can see that he seems to be blinking in slow motion. Henry puts this down to the effects of making the weight, even though he'd been drinking fluids and eating normally for over twenty four hours since the weigh in. But that might not have been the only reason Wharton didn't seem 'switched on'. The fight was almost cancelled that afternoon, and if the reason had been substantiated, the York man would have had more than the loss of his purse to worry about.

Henry and Gary had been sitting in their hotel room passing away the hours before the fight, when in walked a rather distraught looking Mickey Duff. They both knew Duff well enough by now to realise that something was badly amiss. "The fight's off Henry, they've found a problem with you're brain scan." Wharton was waiting for the humorous punchline, but realised within seconds that his manager wasn't joking. Duff said that whoever had inspected the scan at the Board had found an abnormality near the base of the skull.

While Mickey Duff's thought processes might have been in turmoil with regard to the promotion that night, Henry was more concerned with what they'd found and the long term effect on his health. Once all three calmed down from the initial shock, Henry demanded that Duff contact the Board again and ask to have a review of the finding.

An hour or so later, and we can only speculate as to what was going through the fighter's mind, Duff returned with the good news. The doctor at the Board had sought out Wharton's previous brain scans and compared them. He saw they were unchanged, and that what had been thought as a 'new' lesion, was in fact a permanent feature and he was at no greater risk of brain damage than anyone else. A very unsettling experience to say the least!

If the weight and the scan scare were issues for Wharton it didn't show, because this turned out to be a tremendous performance. In the first round both boxers looked sharp with Wharton following the circling Storey with both landing good punches, but the more powerful shots came from Wharton. At the start of the next round Storey began landing cleanly with his jab but Henry switched to southpaw midway through, and loading up with his left, was causing Storey difficulty with heavy punches landing to the head and body. Storey was forced to trade, and was coming off second best in the exchanges. The third round saw Wharton switching stance regularly but was relying on single punches and taking too long to get them off, allowing Storey, who had an excellent jab, to land often. Storey's right eye was cut in this round.

It was turning into a really good fight and few could have anticipated a quick ending. Within twenty seven seconds of the next round Storey was on his back in the corner being counted out following a right hand and a left hook to the top of the head. A magnificent finish which clearly pleased Wharton and his corner men. In the interview for ITV at ringside after the fight, Duff's partner Terry Lawless suggested that Wharton would be fighting Frederic Seillier in January, as he was the mandatory contender for the European title. Duff enthused over the performance and said that Wharton was 20% better than he'd been when he fought Benn and Eubank.

It was not all a bed of roses that night. There were real issues with the arrangements at the Leisure Centre. The Wharton fight didn't start until 11.40pm due to the demands of ITV necessitating a fifty minute delay between the penultimate fight and the main event. There was a lack of toilet facilities for the huge crowd and lack of stewarding at ringside.

Gary Atkin draws an unusual analogy with how Henry was feeling in the days after the fight in relation to his weight making difficulties. "Every fight Henry had, from Benn onwards, he had a tremendous battle with the scales. It was horrible watching him struggle to make 12st. Each time he made the weight we both said 'never again.' But it's like a woman having a baby. Immediately after the birth she'll say, 'that's the last I'm having,' but a few months later her attitude changes. It was the same with Henry. After he won his fights he just decided he'd do it again." Many mothers might disagree with the comparison, but he makes a good point.

There wasn't going to be too much of a break after the Storey fight in November and the proposed contest with Seillier. The fight with the Frenchman should have been ideal for Wharton as a win would lift him back into the number one spot. Henry had seen clips of Seillier and knew his style would suit him. He was confident and looking forward to the fight. Then at the last minute Seillier pulled out with an injury, and in stepped another tall southpaw, Vincenzo Nardiello.

This would be Wharton's third European title fight in six months, an extremely demanding schedule by anyone's standard. Although Henry was perfectly happy when the fights were arranged, given that he'd continue earning good money, and it would keep him in contention for another crack at the world title, we have to ask what was going through Mickey Duff's mind. He could quite easily have taken easier fights in the North Yorkshire area without taking too big a hit financially. It may have been that as these fights had been covered live on television, the TV companies were insisting on championship fights. It's unlikely, even though Seillier was the mandatory contender, that the European Boxing Union would have insisted on all these defences in such a short period of time. Perhaps Duff, knowing Wharton's weight making problems, felt he had to keep him in the gym and fighting regularly to give him the best chance of remaining in the super middle weight division.

To emphasise the weight issue, after the Storey fight, Henry lashed out £550 to buy Avery scales so he could accurately monitor his weight on a daily basis. Four days before the Nardiello fight Wharton weighed 12st 6lb. He'd been training daily for weeks on end and eating nothing but the right food. He was already starting to look gaunt and pale and yet he'd still almost a stone to lose. Nevertheless the weight had been coming down and he felt reasonably confident he'd make it come the time. On the day of the weigh in Wharton and Atkin travelled to Halifax and arrived a couple of hours early so they could have a 'trial' on the scales before the officials appeared.

When Wharton stood on the scales he weighed around 12st 4lb. He was in a state of shock. As he says, "I had nothing left, I was gone. I was completely gone. I had been drained of everything. If someone had stuck a knife in me nothing would have came out. I thought, 'I can't do it, I can't do it.' I'd eaten nothing, I'd drank nothing and I thought it's impossible to lose any more."

They went to a friends pub called the Stump Cross, which had a gym above it, and with his wet suit on, Henry started to go through his exercises to lose the extra poundage. They went back to the Leisure Centre and Henry was still over weight. Wharton remembered how he felt at that point. "I was so exhausted I couldn't even have skipped. I went and lay on the sauna floor with my sweat suit on and I could only stand it for a minute because I was struggling to sweat as I was so dehydrated. I would shadow box when I came out and then went back in. I was shaking and trembling and all the time the clock was ticking. I thought I was going to pass out. I went back to the scales and I was still a pound and a half over and had to put all the wet clothes back on and start again. Eventually came the official weigh in and I made it. But I was ill, I can still remember how I felt to this day."

Arguably Nardiello was probably Wharton's toughest opponent, up to that point, excluding Benn and Eubank. The Italian had won twenty eight of thirty two fights with sixteen of his opponents failing to hear the final bell. For the last four years many of his fights were against a 'who's who' of the world's best at super middle weight. In December 1991 he lost to Victor Cordoba for the WBA title. In his next fight he beat former Wharton sparring partner Troy Watson. In December 1992 he beat Fidel Smith to win the European title and a year later he defended successfully against former Wharton foe, Mauro Galvano. The big fights kept coming for Nardiello. He lost his European crown by knockout to Seillier and two fights later was stopped in eight rounds by Nigel Benn for the WBC title. Two fights after his bout with Wharton, Nardiello would eventually wear the world crown when he beat Sugar Boy Malinga.

In the build up to the fight Henry had been using his friends, Denzil Browne and Michael Gale for sparring but when Seillier pulled out, Darren Ashton was added. This was excellent preparation and in terms of training alone the camp could not have gone better. The only problems surrounded his weight.

On 13 January Henry was again back at the Northbridge Leisure Centre, with a full house and strong backing from his army of supporters, very few of whom had any idea of his problems making the weight. ITV televised the fight.

It quickly became apparent to those in the know that Wharton was badly affected by his weight problems, and faced with a world class boxer, who was clearly up for the task, he was soon in trouble. For the first three rounds Nardiello, from a long solid southpaw stance, was jabbing his way in before launching barrages of straight left hands which consistently rocked Henry's head back. Wharton hardly threw anything in response, and was being systematically taken apart. The Italian was growing in confidence and must have sensed he was en route to a shock victory.

The situation got worse for Wharton in the second half of the third round when a left hand put him down for the first (and, as it turned out, only) time in his professional career. Henry got himself onto one knee and looked over to his corner. He wasn't hurt and timed the count perfectly, getting up as the referee reached eight. At the end of this round most people would have had Nardiello up 30 – 26.

The weight weakened Wharton must have known he was staring defeat in the face, and came out determined to turn things around. At long last he gritted his teeth and took the fight to Nardiello, forcing the Italian to cover up on the ropes. But he couldn't sustain the attacks, allowing his opponent to get back into his rhythm and land his long left hands again. At best Henry might have shared this round.

The fifth was a big one for Wharton. He'd turned the contest from a boxing match to a fight, and this suited him more than Nardiello. It was as good a round of boxing as fans could see anywhere. Both gave it everything and had the ringside spectators on their feet throwing punches with them. As the round drew to a close Wharton landed a big left hook and as the bell sounded a late punch caused Nardiello to briefly collapse on the floor pretending to be hurt. The referee was having none of it and ushered him to his corner. It was noticed that Nardiello was cut under his right eyelid and his corner men worked feverishly to get it under control. When they came out for the next round, after a brief exchange, the eye opened up and the referee summoned the ringside doctor to inspect it. It was a bad one and the fight was stopped, provoking a furious outburst from the Italians.

Atkin can recall the immediate aftermath of the fight while the boxers were still in the ring. "After the fight ended Nardiello comes and says something to Henry and I know this sounds childish but Henry's telling me to cut the gloves off, and what makes me laugh because Nardiello doesn't understand English, but Henry's saying to him , 'me and you, out in the car park,' and Henry's trying to pull the gloves off with his teeth and he's repeating, 'I'll see you in the car park.' Then it calmed down, it was just the adrenalin from the fight."

We can take two different views on the unsatisfactory ending to the Nardiello fight. On the one hand, Henry was definitely suffering from having to lose weight at the very last minute, but was starting to come into the fight, possibly drawing the fourth and winning the fifth, and we know he usually came on strong the longer fights lasted. Could he have overcome the Italian, either stopping him or closing the points gap. On the other hand Nardiello was well ahead at the stoppage and didn't seem to be tiring, or indeed, losing confidence in any way.

The cut, when seen up close, was a 'show stopper'. He couldn't have continued with it. As mentioned previously Nardiello did go on to win the WBC title and a re-match with Wharton for that crown would have been a fight worth seeing.

CHAPTER 13

Working Towards Another Chance

With his victory over Nardiello, Wharton was still in world title contention, and even though Gary Atkin was sure his days as a super middle were over, Mickey Duff was still pursuing another crack at the world championship at that weight. Henry's position was undoubtedly to get another chance at a world crown, and if he'd to make super middle again to do it, then he'd move heaven and earth. It might not be good for his health, but it would certainly boost his bank balance and help towards fulfilling his lifetime's ambition.

The super middleweight picture was confusing, as we've come to expect. In March Steve Collins was scheduled to defend his WBO crown, while Benn, would also defend the WBC version against Sugar Boy Malinga. The IBF and WBA titles were firmly under the control of Americans, with Frankie Liles the WBA champion, and Roy Jones holding the IBF belt. An added problem was the fact that there was no doubt that the EBU were pushing for Wharton to defend against Frederic Seillier.

Running alongside these issues was the knowledge that Wharton's contract with Duff was up for renewal. Henry, after discussions with Gary Atkin, had decided he would be leaving Duff, although he'd given little thought about who'd replace him. Duff and Wharton had never fallen out, and Henry had always trusted him. However, he felt let down with regard to the situation surrounding the fight with Sam Storey when the British title had suddenly been taken off the agenda and was concerned that Duff may not have the power he once had.

Atkin and Wharton travelled down to London to meet Duff on 6 March and used the journey to prepare a speech outlining Henry's decision. They knew it was going to be awkward on two accounts. Firstly, Henry was still a relatively young man and still had Duff on a sort of boxing pedestal. Secondly, they knew Duff was not expecting this decision and would try to use all his worldly wiles to convince Wharton not to leave. They arrived at Duff's offices in Wardour Street with some trepidation, but Wharton stuck to his guns and told his manager that he wouldn't be renewing their contract.

Atkin can remember being stunned at Duff's response. He said the hard bitten old pro was on the point of tears and seemed to have been totally unprepared for this possibility. Once he recovered his composure he made all sorts of promises about what he was going to do for Wharton in the future, almost pleading with Henry to re-consider. In the face of this emotional argument Henry agreed to return to York and let Duff know the final decision the next day. Henry's heart strings were well and truly plucked, and relenting, he signed a new two year contract. However, one of the first things Duff persuaded him to do was to relinquish his European belt so as not to face a trip to France to fight Seillier, with the understanding that all Duff's efforts would be focussed on getting a world title opportunity as soon as possible.

Henry at this time had a more pleasant event to celebrate. He was now with the love of his life, Amanda, and living in the outskirts of York, at Skelton. On 23 March along came their first child, Billy. As the future would reveal Henry and Amanda had entered into a family agreement whereby any sons would be named by Henry and any daughter named by Amanda. Sounds a sensible arrangement, which would be put to good use on a further five occasions!

Meanwhile Duff organised another outing for Wharton on 4 June, back in York, against a French light heavyweight, Stephane Nizard. This arrangement seemed to fly in the face of the promises the manager had been making and would not bring a world title fight any nearer. But we shouldn't blame Duff too much because circumstances outwith his control were conspiring against him. In March, much to everyone's surprise, the unheralded South African, Sugar Boy Malinga, beat Nigel Benn, causing two things to happen. Firstly, WBO holder Steve Collins's management immediately negotiated a lucrative deal to fight Benn, and on the same night in July, at the same venue, Wharton victim Nardiello somehow got a shot at Malinga for the WBC version. This effectively froze Duff and Wharton out of the equation.

This was to be Nizard's first fight outside France and in his last contest he'd lost a split decision for his national light heavyweight title. He was a bit better than a journeyman, winning eighteen out of thirty, ten defeats and two draws. With only five wins coming inside the distance he couldn't be considered a big puncher, but at the same time he'd only been halted on four occasions.

The night at the Barbican was an opportunity to keep

Wharton active, keep him in the limelight, continuing to earn, but also a local promotion for stable mates Denzil Browne and Ron Hopley to appear. With Nizard being a light heavyweight there was relief for Henry because he wouldn't have to make the super middleweight limit. He eventually tipped the scales at 12st 8lb. He was fit, had been training as normal, and the only difference in his preparations for this fight was that he didn't have to starve himself and dry out. The bottom line was that he should've been fighting at a higher weight for years.

Nizard, who bore a striking resemblance to Sylvester Stallone, as Rocky Balboa, put up a tremendous show forcing Wharton to fight every minute of every round. Henry landed every punch in the book but couldn't put a dent in the Frenchman's armour. Nizard kept coming forward, landing often, but as his record demonstrated, he wasn't a concussive puncher. At the end of ten tough rounds Nizard looked even more like Rocky Balboa after being punched senseless by Apollo Creed in the Rocky film. Referee Mickey Vann must have been watching a different fight to ringside commentators, Steve Holdsworth and Bob Mee. Vann gave the fight to the local man by five rounds to three, scoring two even, while both Eurosport staff gave all the rounds to Wharton!

This had been a tough night for Wharton, and with fighting at light heavyweight, he'd been unable to stop Nizard, perhaps putting some doubts in his mind about how effective he might be if he moved permanently to the higher division.

Frustratingly, Duff's plan to get Henry another fight for the WBC championship, in all probability against Sugar Boy Malinga, were once again in turmoil when surprisingly the

South African lost to Nardiello by split decision. The added problem with these splintered titles was that every time a contract was signed, there would be option clauses inserted, ensuring that if the champion lost he could claim a re-match. This type of arrangement prevented someone like Wharton getting his opportunity. Duff knew the problems Henry had making the weight, and time was running out.

For decades Duff and his associates enjoyed a considerable level of control over British boxing at the highest level, but his influence was on the wane. Rival promotional groups led by Frank Warren and Barry Hearn were securing lucrative TV contracts, and signing up the top boxers in Britain. Mickey was facing real challenges in terms of getting his boxers tied in for championship contests and Wharton fell into that category.

Having given up his European title, and now seeing a return with Nigel Benn gone for the foreseeable future, Chris Eubank fighting in the Middle East after losing his world crown, and Duff's own fighter Joe Calzaghe holding the British title, a match with Nardiello, the new WBC champion would have seemed the most likely possibility. Out of the blue however, came fellow Brit, Robin Reid. The Runcorn man was on a run of impressive inside the distance victories, and it was he who was nominated to challenge the Italian. Once again Duff and Wharton were frozen out of the world title picture.

Wharton and Duff both knew that he had to keep fighting until his chance came, primarily to ensure his name was still being discussed by the rating committees. Fortunately Henry still held the Commonwealth crown but a defence of that title would necessitate him making the weight again. This latter factor was critical within the Wharton inner circle. As we know it had been a huge struggle for a number of years, and as each weigh in approached, both Wharton and Atkin were increasingly doubtful that he'd make 12st. It was against this background that Duff matched his charge with Australian Rick Thornberry, once again in Halifax, on 23 October.

Thornberry had never fought outside Australia and the only recognisable name on his record was former Wharton victim, Rod Carr, whom he stopped in eight rounds, eighteen months previously. In his fourteen fights he'd lost only once, and was coming down from light heavyweight.

Wharton was still totally focussed on winning the world title and this belief drove him on to push himself to the limits once again to make the weight for the Thornberry fight. He wasn't underestimating the Australian by any means, Wharton was too experienced for that, but his real battle was now with the scales. By the time of the weigh in he was ill, again, and Henry would once more see his mother couldn't bare to look at him even though she'd say, "you're looking good my son! ". He knew she was only trying to keep his spirits up.

A few days before the fight Wharton learned that Robin Reid had beaten Nardiello in Italy, and his initial thoughts were that this would likely lead to another big title chance for him at home in the not too distant future. His hopes were soon dashed however when press reports suggested that Reid would be forced to defend against Sugar Boy Malinga before making any further plans. Not good news for the Yorkshire man.

Once both boxers entered the ring in Halifax, Wharton looked so much bigger than the former light heavyweight who in fact came in two pounds under the stipulated weight. With Henry having enjoyed top level sparring with naturally bigger men in the shape of Denzil Browne and Michael Gale, Thornberry didn't look like he'd pose too many problems, and so it turned out.

Thornberry circled round the outside of the ring with Wharton chasing, and it soon became clear the visitor didn't have the 'big guns' to keep the champion at bay. In the third round a right hand staggered Thornberry and later he was dropped by a left hook, rising at nine. The following round was similar with the challenger touching down again, with cuts appearing under his left eye and between his eyebrows. The fifth, and what proved to be the final round, was another punishing session for Thornberry and he looked in a sorry state.

There are some in boxing who hold the view that a fighter should continue until the final bell, or be stopped sometime earlier by the referee's intervention, regardless of how forlorn their chance of actually winning is, and irrespective of how much punishment they're taking. Others consider it wiser for the fighter to withdraw when all chance of winning has gone, the injuries are mounting, and perhaps a knock out blow is just around the corner.

Although Thornberry's corner claimed he'd damaged an old shoulder injury when they pulled him out between rounds, there was no getting away from the fact that he was facing much more of same punishment he'd withstood for the fifteen minutes the fight had lasted. His corner made a wise decision.

It's worth noting that Thornberry fought on for a further six years, winning ten on the bounce after Wharton, before losing to Joe Calzaghe on points for the WBO title. Three years after that he lost on points in Germany to Sven Ottke for the IBF version, ending his career with twenty seven wins from his thirty two fights. This then puts Wharton's performance into perspective. On the same night Henry's pal Ron Hopley beat Roy Chipperfield on points.

1996 came to a close with Wharton marking time until Robin Reid could defend his title against Sugar Boy Malinga at the start of the year. It eventually transpired that Malinga would be replaced by fellow South African Giovanni Pretorius before Henry got his chance.

CHAPTER 14

Third Time Lucky ???

Mickey Duff (who sadly passed away as this book was being prepared) had been the leading figure in British Boxing from the early 1960s. He was the ultimate all-rounder in that he'd been active in every role in professional boxing – fighter, trainer, cornerman, matchmaker, manager and promoter. He'd contacts all over the world with boxers, managers, matchmakers, promoters and TV executives. He knew the game inside out.

It's an unusual facet of professional boxing in this country that for long periods one particular promotional group comes to dominate. Sydney Hulls was replaced by Jack Solomons, who in turn was ousted by Duff and his associates, and twenty years later Duff himself was facing that challenge. Now it was Frank Warren, and to a lesser extent, Barry Hearn, who were on the up. Duff could no longer sign up all the top boxing prospects. He no longer had total control of the lucrative television rights, and his influence with the world boxing organisations, as well as the British Boxing Board was on the decline. Naturally enough this did not sit well with him, and he resented having to deal with the newcomers.

These issues were now having an adverse effect on Wharton's chances to get the world title fight he so desperately wanted. Duff had always enjoyed a healthy relationship with the WBC but the problem was that their champion, Robin Reid, was promoted by Frank Warren. Wharton and Atkin had become convinced he'd missed out on a title fight for over a year due simply to the fact that Duff couldn't or wouldn't work with whoever was promoting the current champion.

This matter was eventually resolved, and Duff proved he wasn't quite finished, soon after Reid successfully completed his first defence in February. On 25 March Gary Atkin learned Henry would be fighting Reid on 3 May while he was en route to London with Denzil Browne. The news meant that Henry would get a third chance to fulfil his lifetime's ambition, the venue being the Nynex Arena in Manchester.

Having fought two British legends in Nigel Benn and Chris Eubank, and forcing them to perform at their absolute peaks in order to secure wins, Henry was confident that he'd a more than favourable chance to beat Reid. Once again he decided to set up camp in Tenerife and went back to the Garden City Olympus Club in Las Americas.

This time Henry couldn't use Nigel Benn's gym because it was being refurbished, but Peter De Freitas suggested using one owned by John Palmer. Mr Palmer was born in Birmingham in 1950 leaving school fifteen years later. In 1987 he was found not guilty of the Brink's MAT gold bullion robbery. Melted down gold from the robbery had been found in his garden, but he claimed he didn't know it had been stolen. The press had dubbed him 'Goldfinger'. In 2001 he was found guilty of 'masterminding the largest timeshare fraud on record' and jailed for eight years. At the time of his conviction his personal fortune was estimated at £300 million.

Gary Atkin can remember meeting Palmer and being taken

to the gym. "We arrived outside the famous Harley Davidson Bar. You walk through there and at the back, there's a hotel. You go down the steps, and when he opened the door to this gym, well you've never seen anything like it. It was a real boxing gym. It was brand new. All the chains for the punch bags were shining with the chrome, there was a shag pile carpet on the floor, the ring looked as if it'd just been erected, there were steam rooms, the lot, and it have never been used. All the weights were chrome. So I thought this was amazing. They had showers, you could have got a football team in them."

However, after a few weeks using the premises Wharton and Atkin's inquisitive natures almost landed them in bother with the owner. With a laugh Atkin relates the story. "There was door in the gym which had never been opened, and I wondered what was behind it. I had a bunch of keys, so I tried the keys in the lock and it opened. When I opened it up, I couldn't believe my eyes. It was an underground car park. There were Lamborghinis, Rolls Royces, all in air bubbles. There must have been twenty or thirty of them. Vintage cars, millions and millions of pounds worth of cars. I looked up and saw a camera there. I said to Henry come and see this, and he said 'we were told not to go in there'. I said, 'nobody told me.' There were big old Bentleys with huge fenders from the 1920s. So, I shut the door and locked it. We had finished training and went upstairs for an orange juice. We were sitting on the balcony when this Arab came up to us. He said somebody wanted to see us. I told Henry,' it's you he wants to see', and Henry says, 'no, no, it's you he wants to see, Gary'. I tried to get Henry to come with us but he wouldn't move. We went to this complex and it was like something out of James Bond, buttons getting pressed and doors sliding open. I was ushered into this huge office. You could smell the leather. There was this Arab sitting behind a desk and he looked the part and I'm thinking he's seen me looking at the cars. I heard the door behind me sliding shut. He said, 'is everything all right? John's asked we to say that if there's anything you want just let him know.' Honest, I thought I was going to collapse with relief. So I just said, 'how many tickets does he want for the fight?' He says, 'He's only wanting two. He's going to fly into Manchester from Tenerife, watch the fight and then fly straight back in his private jet.' When I got out I pretended all sorts to Henry. I told him he'd put a gun to my head and Henry was for off home. Eventually I had to tell him the truth."

Once again Henry undertook the same training routine he'd used prior to the Eubank fight. Early morning runs around the volcanic landscape surrounding Mount Teide, then into Palmer's gym for shadow boxing, and the usual exercise routines. It was ideal preparation for Wharton and although it was tough he enjoyed it. Andy Flute was brought over from England for sparring and on occasion Gary Atkin would take on the role. Flute was an inspired choice. He was an experienced campaigner, having had thirty fights, winning eighteen. He'd fought for both the British middleweight and Midlands Area super middleweight titles, but more relevant to Wharton, was his fight only twelve months previously with Robin Reid.

On his return to England, Henry was quietly confident that at long last he'd win a world title, and so too was Mickey Duff. In the week leading up to the fight the camps of all the fighters on the bill moved to Manchester, and in the Midland Hotel,

Duff approached Atkin and Wharton with a proposal. He told them he was prepared to bet Frank Warren £50,000 that Henry would win. He suggested Henry and Gary put up £12,500 each, along with his £25,000. They all agreed and at the press conference in the Victoria and Albert Hotel, Duff interrupted Frank Warren and offered him a £20,000 bet on a Wharton victory. Warren immediately upped the offer to £50,000 and both protagonists shook on it. We shouldn't believe that Duff would have taken such a risk unless he was convinced his man would win.

When Robin Reid had his first professional fight, Wharton was already the British and Commonwealth champion. In 1992 he'd won the bronze medal at the Barcelona Olympics and carried that potential into the paid ranks. Twenty four wins and only one draw had followed. Looking back people don't consider Reid as one of the lethal punchers, but at this time, eighteen of his wins had come inside the distance and in fact his last seven fights had ended early. This included his win over Nardiello, which clinched the world title, and his first defence against Pretorious.

The press kit for the fight showed some interesting facts serving to open the debate as to how the fight might progress. In Wharton's favour, he'd gone twelve rounds on five occasions while Reid had never been that distance. How would the champion cope in the later rounds? Wharton had fought four world champions in Benn, Eubank, Galvano and Nardiello. Reid had only fought Nardiello. Reid had taken part in two championship contests compared with Wharton's eleven. Crucially though, Reid had never lost and his confidence was increasing. It had all the hallmarks of an intriguing contest.

Unusually for Henry in terms of fighting for a world title, his fight was not 'top of the bill'. Alongside his fight, Naseem Hamed was fighting Billy Hardy for the WBO and IBF featherweight titles, and Ronald Wright was fighting local man Steve Foster for the WBO light middleweight crown. All the weigh ins were held at the Nynex Arena the day before the fights.

In the afternoon of Wharton's big day, an incident occurred which had a profound effect on him, and may have influenced his performance on the night. There'd been an acrimonious break up between Henry and his partner and mother of his first two children, Anita. Over the previous couple of years things had not been pleasant. However, Henry knew Anita and their two children, Lydia and Henry, would be attending the fight and arranged tickets for them. We should understand that Henry's new partner, Amanda, was also in attendance, and she too would have a ticket.

Quite sensibly it wouldn't have been wise to have the women sitting next to each other, but when Anita discovered that her tickets were not near the ringside, she was far from happy. Atkin and Wharton had bedrooms on the same floor of the Victoria and Albert Hotel and about three o'clock in the afternoon of the fight, the trainer heard a commotion coming from further along the corridor. Just then his phone rang and it was Henry asking him to come along to his room urgently. When Atkin entered the room he saw Anita and the two children. She was screaming, shouting and attacking Henry. The fighter wanted Atkin to try and take his former partner out the room which left the trainer in a really awkward position because he didn't want to interfere in a personal matter. Eventually Anita and the children left, but the event had left it's mark on Wharton, and Atkin knew it immediately. The spark had gone out of Wharton and from that moment onwards he hardly spoke a word to anyone. When they arrived at the Arena they bumped into Duff and the manager realised something was wrong. He asked Atkin about it and the trainer told him it was just pre-fight nerves. As the warm up in the dressing room began, those closest to the fighter knew he just wasn't himself. As they made their way to the ringside Atkin's gut feeling was that Wharton wouldn't win the fight, in complete contrast to how he had felt during the build up.

The champion came out of the blocks quickly and was moving around the ring landing stinging jabs regularly, with Wharton looking slightly off the pace for the first couple of rounds. By the third, Henry was warming up and managing to get inside and let the punches go. After five rounds both ringside commentators for Sky, Ian Darke and Glen McCrory, had the fight dead even with Wharton beginning to look the more likely. At the start of sixth, Reid adopted a southpaw stance and for the first two minutes there was hardly a punch landed by either boxer. Towards the end of the round there were a few brief flurries but there wasn't much in it.

The next three rounds saw Reid just doing enough to sway the judges with crisp left jabs and the occasional right hand counter as Wharton pursued him relentlessly around the ring. Henry was clearly putting everything into the fight now and had no respect, or fear, of Reid's punches even though, as we recall, he'd stopped his recent opponents. But going into the last third of the fight, Reid seemed to be pulling away.

The tenth was a superb round. Wharton started it off looking jaded and it was no surprise when a vicious right cross from Reid almost knocked him off his feet. Wharton showed his resolve however and came storming back forcing Reid onto the ropes. By the end of the round Reid was starting to feel the pace but was still landing with clean shots.

In the penultimate round Henry gave it everything looking for the knockout, but he just couldn't get a clean shot at Reid. He probably did enough to win the round even though Reid landed the cleaner punches. Going into the last round Reid must have known that all he had to do was stay on his feet to win the fight. He skipped round the ring, moving from side to side, throwing out jabs most of which landed. A tired looking Wharton chased after him in desperation but couldn't land the big punch which might have swung the fight in his favour. At the end, judge Ray Solis somehow scored the fight 114-114 (six rounds each), judge Daniel Van de Wiele scored it 117-113 (seven rounds to three, with two drawn) and Richie Davies had it 118-111 (nine rounds to two with one drawn). A majority victory for Reid.

Reid fought on for a further five years, taking part in twenty six fights, winning eighteen and losing eight. He would lose his WBC title to Sugar Boy Malinga seven months later. He lost three further attempts to win recognised world championships to Joe Calzaghe, Sven Ottke and Jeff Lacy.

Henry's view of the circumstances that night have never changed. "Walking back to the dressing room I couldn't believe I'd lost. I still think the fight was a lot closer than some of the judges thought. In fact I was devastated. I was numb inside. My thoughts on Robin Reid haven't changed to this day, he's a good fighter, all his career he was a good fighter, and a gentleman. If you ask him if he could beat me, he would say,'I did'. If you ask me, I would say, 'he did, but he shouldn't have.'

To the neutral observer, Reid won the fight clearly and boxed brilliantly. He was in superb physical condition, very athletic and had his tactics spot on. Sometimes boxers look for excuses after they lose big fights, Wharton doesn't offer any. But there is room to speculate.

All the way through training both Wharton and Atkin were confident that he'd win. Mickey Duff was so confident he'd bet £50,000 on it, and he didn't like to throw money away. So what did Henry mean when he maintains Reid shouldn't have beaten him? Was Wharton weight drained? Had he aged, as a fighter, overnight, or did the row in the hotel bedroom take the edge off his enthusiasm?

CHAPTER 15

The Final Curtain

In the aftermath of the Benn defeat, Wharton was angry at himself for allowing the first four rounds to slip through his fingers but it left him in no doubt he was capable of winning a world title. The Eubank defeat had been a bruising affair but he knew, when looking back he'd pushed his opponent to the very limits of his endurance. Making the weight had been a major issue but there'd been no thoughts of retirement, and while his ambitions received a severe dent, he still believed that if only he could get another chance the dream was still on. The biggest obstacle after the Eubank defeat was getting himself back into the number one slot.

The Reid defeat was different. Making super middleweight had become the main, if not the sole aim during his recent training camps. It had in many ways overtaken the planning and preparation to simply win the next fight. Henry realised that to get a fourth attempt at the world super middle crown he'd have to meet and beat a number of top ten contenders, or perhaps going back to challenge for British and European honours. Wharton believed he still held the Commonwealth title and bizarrely, even though he had no real intentions of defending it, only found out that it was gone when sitting ringside at Wembley, as we learned previously.

Henry took several months off, concentrating on his

domestic life. He was starting to look beyond his boxing career and thinking about his future. He bought land, with a cottage, near Tadcaster just off the main road between York and Leeds and prepared plans to not only develop the house into a much bigger accommodation but to include his own custom designed boxing gym. Of course, he was increasingly attracted to the golf course and most days he'd be swinging a golf club, and fast becoming a decent club player. Wharton could turn his hand to most things and along with family and friends the building work on his new home provided almost full time employment.

Nevertheless, the itch to get back into the ring soon returned and he was in no doubt his future lay in the next weight division, light heavyweight. There were matters he had to resolve however. As well as boxing at a different weight he felt that a complete change would be beneficial. His managerial contract with Mickey Duff didn't expire until March 1998, and even though he didn't have any real complaints about the way his career had been handled, he realised that Duff was losing his influence, and asked if the contract could end early. There was a bit of sadness on both sides, but Duff agreed, and an amicable separation ensued.

James Russell. who'd worked with Mickey Duff had now moved on to Panix Promotions who looked after world heavyweight champion, Lennox Lewis. Russell contacted Gary Atkin and arranged a meeting between him, Henry and Lewis's manager Frank Maloney. A deal was struck with Maloney whereby Henry would fight on the same bills as Lewis. Henry thought if he could get on the undercard of Lewis's fights, particularly in America, it would bring him to the attention of world governing bodies and might move him into the light heavyweight rankings far quicker. It seemed a sensible strategy.

Wharton knew that Lewis would be fighting Shannon Briggs on 8 March in Atlantic City, so he began his training camp with that in mind. This time he'd be training right outside his front door, at his own gym, and helping him with his sparring was the Lincolnshire heavyweight, Chris Woollas. Although Woollas would become much heavier, at that time he was fighting around the top reaches of the cruiserweight division, and an ideal partner for Wharton.

The original opponent was to have been Roland Pelt from Maryland. He'd won eight in a row before losing his last two. Pelt pulled out and indeed never fought again. His replacement was Franklin Edmondson from North Carolina and looking at his record Wharton would have been thinking it was an ideal baptism. With nine wins from seventeen fights and having lost his last two in a row, both inside the distance, he looked like someone who might give Henry a few rounds, make him look good to his new audience, and provide him with the opportunity for an impressive finish. Edmondson forgot to read the script!

Henry and Gary left for Atlantic City on 23 March, in possession of new boxing shorts in red, white and blue designed by young Gavin Orrey from Acomb who'd won a competition put forward by the sports company, Mizuno. They were in a light hearted mood, and intended enjoying the experience. Although Henry had fought in Poland, Greece, Czechoslovakia and, indeed, New Jersey, as an amateur, he surprisingly had never fought abroad as a professional. Recalling the armed robbery the last time Wharton and Atkin had been in America, it might not have been a surprise that this trip didn't run smoothly either. Along with Terry Lawless and his wife they left Gatwick en route to New York, but halfway across the Atlantic a poor chap at the rear of the plane took a heart attack and the pilot decided to turn back. The aircraft had to fly low to evacuate fuel and when it touched down back in London it was pursued along the runway by fire engines. Wharton was a nervous wreck by the time they turned round to make their way back. During the flight Wharton and Atkin arranged for Terry Lawless to assist them in the corner during the contest.

Once in Atlantic City, the group were accommodated at Caesars Palace where there were good training facilities for the boxers. The last few days of preparation went well but there was some confusion at the weigh in. Henry came in at 12st 9lb, just inside the contracted limit, but Edmondson weighed well over. The Wharton camp demanded he at least got down to 13st, and with some reluctance the Americans eventually agreed. When they entered the ring Edmondson looked more like a cruiserweight and the extra poundage made all the difference. For the first couple of rounds Wharton looked in good form but although he was landing cleanly the local man didn't budge an inch. In the third, a thundering left hook caught Edmondson and he briefly staggered forward into the ropes before regaining his balance. Discouragingly for Wharton that punch would have stopped the vast majority of his super middleweight opponents. Perhaps a little disheartened, Henry struggled during the next two rounds, and the Sky commentary team, possibly influenced by the fact Edmondson was still standing and fighting back, thought that the local man sneaked at least a share of those rounds.

From the sixth onwards Wharton moved into a different gear, up on his toes, throwing quick one-twos and Edmondson looked as if he'd shot his bolt. At the end of each round the American shuffled back to his corner looking exhausted and when the scores were announced by Michael Buffer, Henry had won every round on two of the judges cards.

Wharton had once again injured his left hand, and this may have explained why after the fifth round his tactics changed. Back in York he got the hand x-rayed and although there were no broken bones, there was a build up of damaged tissue which prevented him going straight back into a training regime.

When Wharton looked around at his situation within the light heavyweight division he could see no quick route to a world title attempt. Roy Jones was a virtual super star in America and held two portions of the world title. Dariusz Michalczewski was unbeaten holding another version, but fought solely in Germany. Reggie Johnson, another American, held the IBF title and it was obvious that his people would be vying for a lucrative money spinner against Jones. The doors were closing, or indeed, they were firmly shut.

Domestically there were interesting possibilities. A fortnight before the Edmondson fight fellow Yorkshire man Crawford Ashley won the British title, and the Commonwealth one had just been vacated. This sparked press speculation that Henry's next fight would be in York against Ashley. The problem for Wharton was that although he had an arrangement with Frank Maloney for him to promote his fights, he wasn't his manager.

So while Mickey Duff previously would have been scouring the country trying to arrange deals for his fighter, Henry no longer had this driving force behind him. We have to remember that Maloney controlled the world heavyweight championship through Lewis, and this kept him busy.

It's worthwhile examining what was happening in Wharton's mind as his boxing career was starting to wind down. Up until the Reid fight his whole life revolved round boxing. It was the priority and nothing was allowed to get in the way of his boxing commitments. Like many sportsmen then and now, he'd difficulty considering a life outside the ring. Henry had family and friends who gave him private advice about investing and preparing for the future but when he thought about what they were saying he virtually had nightmares. He simply didn't want to think about a life without boxing. With the long delay after the Reid fight, Henry had for the first time since he was in his early teens, saw another side to life. It wasn't a conscious decision to put his boxing career to one side, it just happened.

As we know his new house had been extended upwards and outwards, with his gym attached. He was meeting people to discuss how he was going to invest his money. He was looking around for some type of business which he could get himself into, to occupy his time, and when his fight in Atlantic City appeared on the horizon, the absolute commitment to training had diminished. If he happened to have a meeting arranged with an accountant, or a lawyer, or a planning official then training was cancelled. Likewise, Gary Atkin had his life to lead and if he too had other meetings arranged, the training once again was pushed aside.

Wharton wasn't stupid, of course he fought for pay, but it wasn't his goal. His aim was always to be a world champion. When he fought Edmondson it wasn't simply to earn more money, for him it was the first step on the road to a world title. He enjoyed fighting in America, he enjoyed not being the centre of attention, and he thought he fought well. But, once back in York, the injured hand, the distractions in his life, he was beginning to realise that his boxing career might be coming to an end. While Maloney was suggesting fights in York and possibly appearing again on a Lewis undercard, Henry was giving serious thought to retiring.

A major distraction for Wharton was a new venture he was planning, as far removed from boxing as anyone could imagine. Henry was intent on opening a Fish and Chip shop at 49 Blossom Street in his home town. This was a very central location, just outside the city walls and coincidently close to his mothers house. The difficulty was that the local residents felt there was an over provision of fast food outlets in the vicinity and Henry had to go through several loops before the Council granted permission.

Meanwhile Lennox Lewis's next defence had been arranged for 26 September in Connecticut and Maloney, while originally wanting Wharton to travel out to America and fight on the same bill, organised a show at the Barbican in York . The Barbican side of things turned into a huge affair with a total of thirteen fights headed by Crawford Ashley boxing Mohamed Siluvangi for the vacant European title, and Paul Ingle taking on Billy Hardy for the European and Commonwealth featherweight crown. Of course, the biggest ticket seller was Wharton.

Henry was a reluctant participant. While he'd been contemplating retirement, he'd bump into friends who would ask when his next fight was happening. Others reminisced about great nights in the past and tell him he'd be the champ at the higher weight. There'd be times when the old urge would return and he'd go out a run and feel as fit as he'd ever been. When Maloney came up with a firm offer for a fight on 26 September, especially as it was planned for the Barbican, he found himself unable to refuse. Typically for Wharton, once he'd made the decision, he realised there was no way he could enter the ring in front of his own fans and give anything less than his best. More importantly, Henry was a winner, and personal pride wouldn't allow a defeat to enter his mindset.

Once again, it was back to the grindstone. The running shoes were looked out, the hand wraps applied, and the weight watching began. As the fight neared, the usual 'fire in the belly' was nothing more than a burning ember. He'd often think to himself, "what am I doing? Why did I agree to this?"

His opponent was Ukrainian, Kostiantyn Okhrei, who'd won eighteen of thirty three fights. Okhrei was improving however and had won four of his last six fights. He was recognised in the trade as someone who didn't go down easily. There were one or two reasonably familiar names on his record. In 1991 he'd gone to Australia and knocked out former Commonwealth champion, Lou Cafaro. Six years later he visited Britain for the first time, losing by sixth round knockout to Dominic Negus in London, and the previous April lost in the fourth to Darren Corbett in Belfast. Without being unkind to the visitor he wasn't as good as Edmondson and should have presented little problem to an in form Wharton.

Wharton weighed 12st 10lb, with the visitor a pound heavier but Henry didn't look as finely cut as he'd been previously. Like the Edmondson fight, the first three rounds were a war, and while exciting for the fans, it wasn't the shrewdest of tactics because Okhrei was as tough as they come. Wharton didn't seem as sharp as he should have been, and of course, we now know why. He was missing wildly in the fourth and was almost bowled over by a thundering right hook. The fans at ringside could hear Wharton shouting to himself in frustration.

Again, similarly to Edmondson, the four rounds had taken their toll on Okhrei, and at the start of the fifth the Ukrainian was feeling the pace. At long last Wharton got his rhythm and Okhrei suffered. A left to the body softened him up and left and rights put him down. It looked like Mickey Vann was going to stop the fight but he allowed it to continue. The sixth, Wharton's last as it turned out, couldn't have been more fitting. The crowd were on their feet screaming for their man and the Henry of old appeared. He threw everything at his opponent and after a head clash, a vicious left hook floored the visitor. As he was getting to his feet, Wharton was seen wiping blood from a badly cut right eye and this had obviously enraged him. Vann waved them together and five consecutive left hooks from Wharton ended the fight – and his career. The Barbican was bedlam as Terry Lawless tried to stem the flow of blood from Wharton's injury, which would need five stitches to close it.

Wharton could be heard screaming at no one in particular. Perhaps it was from frustration as he knew he'd struggled with an opponent who he should have seen off far quicker. Perhaps it was simply due to the badly cut eye, something that had never happened to him before. Looking back now Henry can remember his thoughts. "I just wasn't there. I was even sitting in the corner before the bell went and I was looking around thinking, 'I'm lost, what am I doing here?' I don't know if it was because I'd lost my third world title attempt and I thought I was going to win, and I couldn't come to terms with it all. It scarred me. I had nightmares about it."

Besides Henry and his trainer nobody knew what his mindset had been coming up to the Okhrei fight. The explosive finish, the adulation of the York crowd, and the aggressive outburst excited promoters and television producers. With Crawford Ashley also claiming the European title to add to his British and Commonwealth belts, a 'local derby' between them for the 'triple crown' was an obvious money spinner. Within days the local press were discussing a November date in Leeds with Gary Atkin suggesting Headingley cricket ground as the venue.

Even though Henry's heart was no longer in it, when big money is on offer it's hard to turn it down. He thought that once the fight was arranged the old motivation would return and he'd settle down into the usual routine. Before training could get underway good news arrived in the shape of a positive report from York planning department for his Fish and Chip shop and shortly after 7 October the premises started trading.

The upturn didn't last long because Wharton's eye injury didn't heal as expected. When he visited a specialist it was discovered that the eye had healed from the outside leaving a space underneath which simply hadn't knitted together. A single punch could have sliced the skin open and on 13 October there was no alternative but to cancel the fight. Panix Promotions had already fixed a date for the 21 November at Hull Arena.

As far as everyone was concerned this was simply a delay, and before long a new date, 6 February, was settled upon, this time back at North Bridge Leisure Centre in Halifax. Gary Atkin had taken the bold step of making this a joint promotion between him and Maloney. There was even talk that Don King would be coming over to run the rule over Wharton with a view to him fighting the WBA champion, Reggie Johnson. As far as the public were concerned it looked like an opening for another run at a world championship for Henry.

However, that idea was not playing out inside Wharton's head. Not only was the fire not burning in his belly, there wasn't even a spark. He simply couldn't find the urge to commit to a rigorous training schedule. In an effort to find the inspiration he went up to Sunderland in the hope that being around other boxers in Billy Hardy's gym might encourage him. One night Henry was sitting in a guest house in Washington, Tyne and Wear after a training session. He'd been feeling a bit depressed, was alone, with Amanda and the children back at home. He thought back to the Okhrei fight and realised it was only when the Ukrainian was landing really hard punches that he began to respond and put his heart and soul into the fight. He asked himself what had his boxing career come to, when he'd to take heavy punches before he felt like fighting?

Sitting in that darkened room up in Washington, Wharton made the decision that his career was over. He phoned Amanda, his dad, and his mother, and told them his decision. Neither put up an argument. Henry got into his car, rolled the window down, and drove back to York a very happy man. The pressure was off. No more watching what he was eating, no more missing out on a night at the pub, and no more fretting about injuries. No more getting up out of bed to run in the rain, and sparring, when all he was doing was going through the motions. The next day he phoned his friend Gary Atkin and gave him the news.

On 13 January Wharton announced his retirement, and the fight with Ashley was off.

CHAPTER 16

Life Goes On

It has always been matter of some interest what a top sportsman does once he retires. If he happened to be a top class footballer, and either becomes well known in the media, or manages a top level club, then he remains very much in the public eye. Other retired stars appear occasionally in our newspapers for a whole variety of reasons, not always favourable. For the vast majority however they tend to lead a fairly mundane and routine sort of life, and might find it difficult to understand why former fans might like to know what they'd done in retirement.

Many find that for a few years they're recognised when out and about, but this gradually fades over time, and while to some that comes as a relief, others can get depressed feeling that their fame has evaporated. Nevertheless, there is an appetite among those fans who supported these sportsmen to know just what happened to their former heroes.

When Henry retired at the age of thirty in early 1999, he'd become a minor celebrity in his home town of York, and featured regularly in the local press. He'd also become a well known face among the travelling community who were proud of his success and the favourable image he'd created for them. Remember, it was estimated Wharton had taken around 8,000 fans to Manchester for the Eubank fight and many of those had memorable experiences through the years supporting him wherever he went. They missed those nights and it was no surprise that for over a year, there were persistent rumours about a Wharton comeback.

There were promoters and managers who recognised Henry's fan base, and thought a return would be financially worthwhile. In July press reports stated that Henry was missing boxing and was considering a comeback. Another York based boxer, Jamie Warters, had appeared on the scene and this provoked speculation a match could be made. In January 2000 there were reports that Wharton and Atkin were in talks with Frank Maloney about a comeback and even suggestions he'd fight Londoner, Mark Delaney, in an eliminator for the British title. Neither Henry nor Gary have any recollection about any of this.

In the meantime the shop was doing well and a real family concern with Henry and Amanda working long hours to ensure its success. Henry also had time to perfect his golf swing at the local Fulford club where his handicap was down to twelve. On 13 May he took his boxing success onto the links when along with partner, Nigel Lewis, they won the York Union of Golf Clubs Kitching Trophy at Kirbymoorside.

By the following spring, the boxing bug was back, but not to the point of actually entering the ring himself. His cousins, George and Reg Robshaw, had turned professional and were training at the gym attached to Henry's house. The old team of Henry and Gary were back on the scene and took the brothers all over the country for their fights. George had seven bouts, winning six and drawing the other. Reg won four and lost two, but both suffered from inactivity, sometimes going a year between fights.

Around this time Henry made up his mind to have his own boxing gym in York and not simply relying on the one he had at his home. With this in mind, and given the fact the long hours at the Fish and Chip shop were taking their toll, he decided to sell up. The premises were put up for sale at £169,500 (£237,000 at 2013 values).

In October 2001, disaster struck. Henry admits, with embarrassment, that he was stupid and deserved his punishment. Late one evening, after a night drinking at home, he drove into Tadcaster and was stopped by the police. He was two and a half times over the drink driving limit and banned for two years. This was a big issue for him at the time because he was still being invited to events, mostly at night, which meant he'd to burden friends and relatives for lifts.

With the shop sold Henry began the search for a place to build his boxing gym but nothing seemed to be suitable. By this time he was working with a family roofing and window fitting company, but still found time in May 2004 to win the local Lewis Trophy along with Adam Newton, with his handicap now down to ten.

The Wharton family had continued to grow. By 2007, Billy junior had been joined by Oscar, Lyla, Sonny, Maddison and Jersey. As we already know, Henry and Amanda had arrived at a novel idea for naming the children. All sons' names would be chosen by Henry and Amanda would do the same with the girls. Guess who Oscar and Sonny were named after?

Out of all the family, Henry's brother Eddie, had been the foremost supporter of his boxing career. We know he'd often sparred with Henry and Ron Hopley in the basement of the family home when his professional career was just starting out, and it was a time of great sadness in January 2006 when Eddie passed away after a short illness, at the relatively young age of only forty four.

Henry never gave up on his overriding ambition of having his own boxing gym and in December 2011 secured part of the old Regent Cinema in Acomb. These were huge premises. If we can imagine looking at the side of a traditional cinema and drawing a horizontal line half way up the wall. The upper portion would become the gym with the lower portion rented out as office space.

Over the next twelve months Henry and his friends worked like beavers to prepare the building. There was flooring work needing done, work on the walls, a new internal roof, re-wiring, the creation of office space and decorating before installing the boxing equipment could begin. All of this costs money and it was a great help when Scunthorpe business men, Dean Sherriff and Mark Stanley of Empire Tapes, plus others stepped in to help with sponsorship. As it was approaching completion Nigel Benn even took time to make a visit while in the area on a promotional tour. One sad point for Henry during the refurbishment was the death of his first trainer, Bill Brown, who passed away in the April. Henry would have loved to have shown the new gym to him, and in fact, he'd intended asking Bill to be a coach.

After a few false starts the gym was officially opened on 21 January 2013 with Henry being assisted by his old friend Ron Hopley as well as Tony Murray and Reece Morrill. It has everything, and more, that would be expected in a modern boxing gym. Two full sized rings, scores of heavy bags, plenty of space for ground work, mirrors to perfect technique, toilets and showers. 'Henry's gym' as it is called even has it's own website. A coffee shop and office accommodation complete the 10,000 square feet of space.

Wharton's life has now come almost full circle. He started out as a young teenager at the York Amateur Boxing Club, and over thirty years later he's now back at a York boxing club, only this time he's the coach on the look out for the next champion. He's still a well known face in the area, swinging his clubs regularly with friends, and doing the odd roofing job. He can socialise in York with the same people he's drank with for decades, testament to his easy-going personable nature which has never been effected by fame and fortune. Ron Hopley is still around after twenty five years, coaching with others at the gym three nights a week. Gary Atkin and Henry can pick up the phone and speak to each other as if not a moment has passed since they were travelling off to Tenerife and America preparing for fights half the country were anticipating.

They're are regrets of course. Henry hadn't been in touch with Mickey Duff for years but both himself and Gary attended their old mentor's funeral in early spring 2014. Even then Henry's innocence shone through. Duff was Jewish, and at his funeral those attending were asked to wear the traditional skull caps. When our two Yorkshire men arrived, they noticed former boxer, Billy Schwer entering the premises wearing the required headgear which prompted Henry, not yet aware of the custom, to remark, "Gary, I didn't know Billy Schwer was Jewish!"

But it was the estrangement with his old friend and coach,

Terry O'Neill, which causes Henry his biggest concern. Their formal relationship seemed to have ended amicably enough after the Benn fight, but circumstances changed over time, and although there was never a bad word uttered by either, they drifted apart. It's easy to understand and accept both perspectives, but that doesn't make it any less sad after all they'd been through together. Terry assisted with the preparation for this book without hesitation and had nothing but warm memories of their time together, as does Henry himself. Maybe it's publication will bring them together?

This will probably not be the end of the Wharton boxing story. It would be nice for Henry and his fellow coaches to find a lad to win the ABA title and represent his country at the Olympic games, thereby exorcising the ghosts which still haunt him. Or maybe even unearth another top class professional capable of landing the ultimate prize, one which eluded Henry on three momentous occasions?

Henry Wharton Fight Record

Date	Venue	Opponent	Result
21.09.89	Harrogate	Dean Murray	W KO 1
25.10.89	London	Mike Aubrey	W Pts
05.12.89	Dewsbury	Ron Malek	W KO 1
11.01.90	Dewsbury	Guillermo Chavez	W KO 1
03.03.90	London	Joe Potts	W KO 4
11.04.90	Dewsbury	Juan Elizondo	W TKO 3
18.10.90	Dewsbury	Chuck Edwards	W KO 1
31.10.90	London	Dino Stewart	W Pts
21.03.91	Dewsbury	Francisco Lara	W KO 1
09.05.91	Leeds	Frank Minton	W KO 7
27.06.91	Leeds	Rod Carr	W Pts
		(Vacant Commonwealth Title)	
30.10.91	Leeds	Lou Gent	Draw
		(Defence of Commonwealth Title)	
23.01.92	York	Nicky Walker	W Pts
19.03.92	York	Kenny Schaefer	W KO 1
08.04.92	Leeds	Rod Carr	W TKO 8
		(Defence of Commonwealth Title)	
23.09.92	Leeds	Fidel Castro Smith	W Pts
	(Defence of Commonwealth Title and Challenge for British Title)		
07.04.93	Leeds	Ray Domenge	W TKO 3
01.07.93	York	Royan Hammond	W TKO 3

07.10.93	York	Ron Amundsen	W TKO 8
26.02.94	London	Nigel Benn	L Pts
	(Challenge for WBC Title)		
10.09.94	Birmingham	Guy Stanford	W KO 3
26.10.94	Leeds	Sipho Moyo	W KO 1
	(Defence of Commonwealth Title)		
10.12.94	Manchester	Chris Eubank	L Pts
	(Challenge for WBO Title)		
08.07.95	York	Mauro Galvano	W KO 4
	(Vacant European Title)		
11.11.95	Halifax	Sam Storey	W KO 4
	(Defence of European and Commonwealth Titles)		
13.01.96	Halifax	Vincenzo Nardiello	W TKO 6
	(Defence of European title)		
04.06.96	York	Stephane Nizard	W Pts
23.10.96	Halifax	Rick Thornberry	W TKO 5
	(Defence of Commonwealth title)		
03.05.97	Manchester	Robin Reid	L Pts
	(Challenge for WBC title)		
28.03.98	Atlantic City	Franklin Edmondson	W Pts
26.09.98	York	Kostyantyn Okhrey	W TKO 6

Record
31 fights, 27 wins (20 inside the distance), 3 defeats, 1 draw.